THE TRAGEDY OF MACBETH

The Tragedy of Macbeth

WILLIAM SHAKESPEARE

EDITED BY R. A. FOAKES
UNIVERSITY OF KENT

THE BOBBS-MERRILL COMPANY, INC.

A SUBSIDIARY OF HOWARD W. SAMS & CO., INC.

INDIANAPOLIS • NEW YORK

First Printing

Copyright © 1968 by The Bobbs-Merrill Company, Inc.

Printed in the United States of America

Library of Congress Catalog Card Number 67–29974

Designed by Joseph P. Ascherl

Cover and Title Page Illustrations by Edward Gorey

The Bobbs-Merrill Shakespeare Series

is under the General Editorship of

Ian Watt, Stanford University

CONTENTS

Introduction

   Macbeth, the Tragedy of Ambition,
     and the Revenge Tragedy   vii

   Macbeth and the Critics   x

   King James I, Witchcraft, and *Macbeth*   xii

   Macbeth in the Theater   xvii

Shakespeare's Text and the Present Edition   xxv

List of Characters   xxix

Text   1

Appendixes

   A A Shakespeare Chronology   157

   B Sources for *Macbeth*   159

   C A Note on Shakespeare's English   172

   D *Macbeth* at the Globe in 1611   175

   E Textual Problems and the Witches' Songs   176

   F Bibliography   179

   G Abbreviations, References, and Editions   182

Illustrations

   Macbeth and Banquo Meeting the Weird Sisters.
     Frontispiece from Holinshed's *Chronicles*   xiii

   Sketch of a London Theater at the
     End of the Sixteenth Century   xix

   Engraving of King James I with London in the
     Background, by Francis Delaram   xx

   Map of Scotland   xxviii

Introduction

MACBETH, THE TRAGEDY OF AMBITION, AND THE REVENGE TRAGEDY

In writing *Macbeth*, Shakespeare transformed to his own ends a mode of tragedy that had been long established. The play is basically a tragedy of ambition, in which is enacted the rise to power and subsequent fall of an aspiring prince. Such a description, while oversimple, serves at one and the same time to suggest both the links *Macbeth* has with medieval tragedy and how far Shakespeare moved beyond its limits.

Medieval tragedy was not so crude as the famous definition of Chaucer's Monk would indicate:

> Tragedie is to seyn a certeyn storie,
> As olde bookes maken us memorie,
> Of him that stood in greet prosperitee,
> And is yfallen out of heigh degree
> Into myserie, and endeth wrecchedly.

The falls of great men were, in fact, treated as Christian moral fables; by showing how Fortune destroys good and bad alike, medieval tragedy encouraged a contempt for the inconstancy of Fortune, as expressed by the Monk in his advice:

> Lat no man truste on blynd prosperitee.

The action of Fortune, setting a man up and then casting him down, was a latent theme in those morality plays which showed mankind, or Everyman, reduced to wretchedness before being finally saved by the intervention of Mercy; and this theme became prominent in the sixteenth century as the morality play developed into the secular interlude. In John Skelton's play *Magnificence* (after 1515; printed 1533), the fall of a great prince was still treated allegorically; but later, and especially after the success of *The Mirror for Magistrates* (1559)—a collection of

vii

poems recounting the downfall of figures from British history—
many plays were written dealing with historical events and people. These plays on historical themes became increasingly concerned with questions of sin, guilt, and retribution, however much
the moral might remain, in the words of the Induction to *The
Mirror for Magistrates*,

> That when thou seest how lightly they did lose
> Their pomp, their power, and that they thought most sure,
> Thou mayst soon deem no earthly joy may dure.
>   (lines 117—19)

Out of the interplay of these and other developments there
came into being, as one mode of tragedy successful on the Elizabethan stage, plays concerned with ambitious princes, and based
on real, or what were then thought to be real, historical personages
and events. Some of these plays, like Shakespeare's *Henry VI*,
portrayed a series of multiple tragedies arising from the miseries
of civil wars, and suggest a political rather than a personal the-
matic interest. Some continued to do little more than show the
rise and fall of a character in terms of Fortune's wheel, turning
from prosperity to defeat that impels an outcry like Edward IV's

> Though Fortune's malice overthrow my state,
> My mind exceeds the compass of her wheel.
>   (3 *Henry VI*, IV.iii.46—7)

Christopher Marlowe, in the first part of *Tamburlaine*, broke
the pattern by showing a hero striding to ever greater conquests,
apparently immune to Fortune's malice, but Shakespeare's early
work suggests that he began with more conventional ideas of the
falls of great men, such ideas as Richard II indicates when, in his
self-dramatizing way, he imagines

> . . . sad stories of the death of kings,
> How some have been deposed, some slain in war,
> Some haunted by the ghosts they have deposed,
> Some poisoned by their wives, some sleeping killed,
> All murdered. . . .
>   (*Richard II*, III.ii.156—60)

The theme of the ambitious prince finally overthrown was developed in several of Shakespeare's plays; it is one of the repeated subjects of *Henry VI*, and becomes dominant in *Richard III*. Richard has no concern for Fortune until he is brought low, but he has no conscience either, and as a tragic figure he belongs much more with earlier patterns of tragic development than with Shakespeare's maturity. For, in creating Brutus in *Julius Caesar*, and then Macbeth, Shakespeare went beyond ideas of Fortune and retribution for crimes committed, to exploit further possibilities in the theme of the ambitious prince. He made his central dramatic concern the growing involvement in evil, the self-deceptions, and the mental torture of a naturally good or even pious man succumbing to temptation, trying to justify himself, and being tormented by his conscience. The play of *Macbeth* was the culmination of a long development of tragic writing on the theme of the rise and fall of an ambitious prince, but it transcends all that preceded it in the subtlety and profundity with which the nature of ambition, and its effects on human character, are explored.

Macbeth also belongs to, but transcends, another long and important dramatic tradition, that of Senecan tragedy. Seneca's plays had begun to be translated from the Latin in 1559; and their highly melodramatic and rhetorical exploitation of the horrors of murder (often of a wicked tyrant) and its gruesome revenge became the basis of much early Elizabethan tragedy. Kyd's *The Spanish Tragedy* (printed 1592) was extremely popular and influential in establishing the conventions of the Elizabethan revenge tragedy, and Shakespeare had used most of its elements in *Titus Andronicus* (1594) and other early works. The heroes of such plays were often, like Richard III, tyrants and "Machiavels," cruel and practiced in deceit, who fascinated the Elizabethan audience by their lusty delight in their own cunning. The exuberant and indiscriminate sensationalism of the early drama was richly if erratically theatrical, but it was the work of a generation of playwrights to tame, extend, and humanize the conventions they inherited. By the time of *Macbeth* the possibilities of this tradition were being much more fully explored and developed—by Shakespeare in such plays as *Hamlet*, and by many of his contemporaries, including Marston, Tourneur, and Chapman. The villain-hero, the long succession of murders, the use of night, madness, and such supernatural elements as mysterious prophecies, ghosts, and other apparitions—all these are the traditional Senecan and revenge elements imaginatively transmuted into a deeper realization of the motives and horror of Macbeth's actions and of the working out of his doom.

MACBETH AND THE CRITICS

Not for a long time did critics of *Macbeth* begin to explore in depth its subtlety and profundity. When critical commentary on *Macbeth*, as on Shakespeare's other plays, began to flourish in the eighteenth century, Macbeth and Lady Macbeth were often seen rather too simply in terms of evil. Thus Dr. Johnson wrote, "Lady Macbeth is merely detested, and though the courage of Macbeth preserves some esteem, yet every reader rejoices at his fall." This view of Macbeth persisted in, for example, Charles Lamb's linking of Macbeth with Iago as one of Shakespeare's "great criminal characters." However, the powerful interpretation of Lady Macbeth from 1777 onward by the actress Mrs. Sarah Siddons—who seemed to William Hazlitt to be "Tragedy personified"—helped to establish the character as a majestic yet ultimately pathetic figure, and so to reveal something of the depth of Shakespeare's creation. Then, in 1785, Thomas Whately made an extended comparison of Macbeth and Richard III in order to show that, unlike Richard, Macbeth's "natural disposition . . . is not bad." This comparison was also used by Hazlitt, who further distinguished Macbeth from Richard; Macbeth is "accessible to pity, is even the dupe of his uxoriousness, and ranks the loss of friends and of his good name among the causes that have made him sick of life." The growing recognition of the complexity of Macbeth as a "character of imagination" is marked in S.T. Coleridge's comments on the way in which Macbeth "mistranslates the recoilings and ominous whispers of conscience into prudential and selfish reasonings, and after the deed, the terrors of remorse into fear from external dangers."

Coleridge looked for consistency in the play as a whole, and he found no justification for the "comedy" of the Porter scene, which he thought was "an interpolation by the actors." It remained for later critics to account adequately for the presence of the Porter. The finest nineteenth-century essay on this aspect of the play is Thomas De Quincey's "On the Knocking at the Gate in *Macbeth*" (1823), in which the knocking is seen as heralding the intervention of ordinary human life upon the "world of darkness" that Macbeth and Lady Macbeth have inhabited while carrying out the murder of Duncan. The general emphasis of criticism was still on character, and this culminated in the famous analysis of the play by A. C. Bradley in his *Shakespearean Tragedy* (1904). He emphasized the sublimity of the two central figures, proud, peremptory, and fired with a passionate ambition to rule. For Bradley the special characteristic of Macbeth as tragic hero was that "this bold ambitious man of action has, within certain limits, the imagination of a poet," suggesting that his contact with the supernatural, and his intimations of conscience, of moral ideas, come to him through images. In this perception, and in Bradley's sense of the play's atmosphere ("a black night broken by flashes of light and colour"), he pointed the way forward to what was to become a particular concern of much twentieth-century criticism: the poetry, imagery, and symbolism of *Macbeth*.

A seminal essay in this respect was that by Caroline Spurgeon in her study of *Shakespeare's Imagery* (1935), where by her meticulous isolation of the imagery of clothing, showing Macbeth as a "small, ignoble man encumbered and degraded by garments unsuited to him," she seemed to offer a new insight into the play. Other critics have pressed this kind of analysis much further, and it is seen in its most subtle and extreme form in the essay by Cleanth Brooks on "The Naked Babe and the Cloak of Manliness" (1947), in which Brooks argued that the idea of child "dominates the symbolism," and that the lines on pity, "like a naked new-born babe" (I.vii.21), are the central passage in the play. The analysis of imagery led also to a concern with the play as a "dramatic poem," and to a study of its themes or ideas. Among the best-known essays on this aspect of the play are those by L. C. Knights: first, "How Many Children Had Lady Macbeth?" (1933), in which Knights, reacting against criticism that concentrated on character, offered a reading of the play through its atmosphere and coloring as a "statement of evil"; and second, the essay in his book *Some Shakespearean Themes* (1959), in which his concern is more with the way that evil is suggested in the play by what is "unnatural" (see, for instance, Act II, scene iv) as opposed to what is "natural," and by the way in which time becomes meaningless for Macbeth (see, for instance, Act V, scene v).

Such criticism has aroused the objection that subtleties of verbal meaning are given an emphasis quite out of proportion to their actual impact on the audience. So it may be argued that few in an audience witnessing *Macbeth* notice the scattered imagery of clothing. Furthermore, such criticism has a tendency to issue in propositions (for example, that the play is a "statement of evil," or that the symbolism of the child is dominant) which the total experience of the action does not support. Criticism which focuses on character is equally liable to give too little weight to the richness of the poetic texture in *Macbeth*, which is, in its language, the most compressed and metaphorical of all the tragedies. Perhaps the main critical problem now is to harmonize the two basic approaches to the play, so that we may come fully to understand how its complexities of language are involved with and contribute to its complexities of character and action.

KING JAMES I, WITCHCRAFT, AND *MACBETH*

In writing *Macbeth*, Shakespeare turned to Scottish history for his material for the first and only time. His main source for the play was the *Chronicles of Scotland* in Raphael Holinshed's *Chronicles of England, Scotland and Ireland* (1577; issued in a

Then Banquho, what maner of women
(faith he) are you, that feeme fo litle fanourable
vnto me, where as to my fellow here, befides
highe offices, yee affigne alfo the kingdome, ap-
pointyng forth nothing for me at all? Yes fayth
the firfte of them, wee promife greater benefites
vnto thee, than vnto him. for he fhall reygne in
in deede, but with an vnluckie ende: neyther
fhall he leaue any iffue behinde him to fucceede

in his place, where contrarily thou in deede fhalt
not reygne at all, but of thee thofe fhall be borne
whiche fhall gouerne the Scottifhe kingdome
by long order of continuall difcent. Herewith
the forefayde women banifhed immediatly out
of theyr fight . This was reputed at the firft
but fome vayne fantafticall illufion by Makbeth and Banquho, in fo muche that Banquho woulde call Makbeth in iefte kyng of

M.ij. Scot-

The Weird Sisters meeting Macbeth and Banquo on the heath, in an
engraving reproduced from Raphael Holinshed's *Chronicles of England, Scotland and Ireland* (1577), page 243 (British Museum copy,
catalogue number 598.G.34). Macbeth and Banquo appear to be dressed
as Tudor gentlemen, and the costumes of the Weird Sisters, though
more exotic, are also recognizably of Holinshed's time. Shakespeare
also probably thought of his characters as costumed according to the
customs of his own age. For Shakespeare's transformation of Holinshed's words and picture into drama, see Act I, scene iii, lines 51–78.

revised and enlarged edition, the one Shakespeare used, in 1587); and out of the stories he found there of the murder of King Duff, the reign of Macbeth, his murder of Banquo and overthrow by Malcolm (see Appendix B), Shakespeare fashioned his tragedy. There is little doubt that he was drawn to a Scottish theme by the coming of King James VI of Scotland to London in 1603, when he succeeded Queen Elizabeth I and began his reign as James I of England.

Companies of actors in the reign of Queen Elizabeth operated under the patronage of a nobleman, for the claim to be his servants and the wearing of his livery might protect the actors from the charge of vagrancy, or the spite of civic authorities, who viewed them as distracting men from work and causing public disturbances. Until Queen Elizabeth died, Shakespeare's own company, performing at the Globe Theatre, had as patron the Lord Chamberlain; then King James and his pleasure-loving Queen Anne took the major acting companies directly under royal protection, and Shakespeare's company became the King's Men, with the right to wear the royal livery. In the years following the accession of James I, the King's Men frequently performed plays at court, especially for winter festivities. There is nothing to associate *Macbeth* specifically with a court performance, but the text contains plenty of evidence, even beyond its general Scottish theme, to connect it with King James.

In the first place, the King was interested in witchcraft. In 1597 he had published a treatise called *Demonology*, in which he affirmed his belief that the Devil makes servants of ignorant or superstitious women, teaches them his arts, and enables them as witches to do all sorts of mischief. Such creatures should be brought to trial, wrote James, and although judges should beware of condemning anyone whose guilt was not certain, all proven witches should be punished with death. "I pray God," the treatise ended, "to purge this country of those devilish practices: for they were never so rife in these parts as they are now." King James had in mind the case of Agnes Sampson, who, with a number of other suspects, was interrogated by him in Edinburgh after a sudden tempest had scattered the fleet bringing his royal bride, Anne of Denmark, to Scotland in 1589. After cruel torture, Agnes Sampson confessed to causing a great tempest at sea which had sunk a boat carrying jewels for Queen Anne, to giving the King "a contrary wind to the rest of his ships" when he sailed from Denmark, and to using the venom of a black toad to practice witchcraft against his life. The affair was commemorated in a little book, *News from Scotland* (1591), and when the King wrote his own *Demonology*, he laid particular stress on the iniquity of practicing witchcraft against a prince.

James himself became less credulous as time went by, but his interest in witchcraft reflected a widespread concern. Although James was not responsible for it, the year after he arrived in London a new statute against witches was brought into force, and witches continued to be executed in England throughout his reign. Some men regarded the common stories about witches as "false and fabulous," and argued so in writing. One such was Samuel Harsnet, whose *Declaration of Egregious Popish Impostures* (1603) provided Shakespeare with the names of the devils that Edgar, as Poor Tom, talks of in *King Lear*. Another was Reginald Scot, whose *Discovery of Witchcraft* (1584) reports at length common beliefs about witches (while treating them with a healthy skepticism), and Shakespeare may have picked up from this work some specific details about witches—their ability, for instance, to keep spirits in the likeness of toads and cats.

If witchcraft was a subject that interested King James, so too was the Scottish history on which the play is based. For according to the *Chronicles*, Banquo was James's own ancestor, and the King could scarcely have failed to be stirred by Macbeth's growing certainty that, as he says,

> For Banquo's issue have I filed my mind;
> For them the gracious Duncan have I murdered;
> Put rancours in the vessel of my peace
> Only for them; and mine eternal jewel
> Given to the common enemy of man,
> To make them kings, the seeds of Banquo kings!
> (III.i.64—9)

These kings appear finally as apparitions, called forth by the Witches (IV.i.110). The prophecy (I.iii.67) by three "Weird Sisters" that Banquo's successors should "govern the Scottish kingdom by long order of continual descent" was recorded in Holinshed's *Chronicles*, and the incident was used by Matthew Gwinn to provide a complimentary address to James when he visited Oxford in 1605. Three figures dressed as *Sibyllae*, or prophetesses, greeted him with a Latin address repeating the Banquo story and foretelling a further long succession for the King's own heirs.

The play has other connections with King James. Some are matters of minor details, such as the reference in II.iii.9, which is almost certainly to the defense of equivocation by the Jesuit Father Garnet during his trial for treasonable complicity in the Gunpowder Plot of 1605, a defense which had excited James's anger; and the passage about "touching for the King's Evil" (IV.iii.146–59), a power of healing scrofula by laying-on of hands traditionally ascribed to royalty, is a reminder that James prided himself on possessing this power. There is also a more general connection, since James had written with some feeling in his advice to his son, *Basilikon Doron* ("King's Gift" [Edinburgh, 1599; London, 1603]) on the subject of the good king and the tyrant:

A good king, thinking his highest honour to consist in the due dis-charge of his calling, employeth all his study and pains to procure and maintain, by the making and execution of good laws, the welfare and peace of his people; and as their natural father and kindly master, thinketh his greatest contentment standeth in their prosperity, and his greatest surety in having their hearts, subjecting his owne private affections and appetites to the weal and standing of his subjects, ever thinking the common interest his chiefest particular: where by the contrary, an usurping tyrant, thinking his greatest honour and felicity to consist in attaining *per fas, vel nefas,* [i.e., by law, or else by crime] to his ambitious pretences, thinketh never himself sure, but by the dissention and factions among his people; and counterfeiting the saint while he once creep in credit, will then (by inverting all good laws to serve only for his unruly private affections) frame the Commonweal ever to advance his particular: building his surety upon his peoples' misery: and in the end (as a step-father and an uncouth hireling) make up his own hand upon the ruins of the Republic. And according to their actions, so receive they their reward. For a good king (after a happy and famous reign) dieth in peace, lamented by his subjects, and admired by his neighbours; and leaving a reverent renown behind him in earth, obtaineth the crowne of eternal felicity in heaven. And although some of them (which falleth out very rarely) may be cut off by the reason of some unnatural subjects, yet liveth their fame after them, and some notable plague faileth never to over-take the committers in this life, besides their infamy to all posterities hereafter. Whereby the contrary, a tyrant's miserable and infamous life, armeth in end his owne subjects to become his burreaux [i.e., hangmen].

All this is not to argue that *Macbeth*, a play very much on the theme outlined here, was written as a compliment to James, or for performance before him, although both these are possible; what the links with King James show is the way in which the coming of James of Scotland to London turned Shakespeare's thoughts to witchcraft and to Scottish history, and stimulated him to write a great play.

MACBETH IN THE THEATER

Clearly, *Macbeth* was written after the accession to the throne of King James I in 1603, and the Porter's apparent reference to the trial of the Jesuit Father Garnet (II.iii), which took place in March 1606, makes it seem likely that *Macbeth* was mainly composed in that year. Some scholars have believed that this allusion was interpolated, perhaps for a court performance of the play when King James entertained King Christian IV of Denmark in July and August, but there is no evidence that *Macbeth* could have been written much earlier. Allusions to the ghost of Banquo in two plays, *The Puritan*, probably by Thomas Middleton (performed in 1606), and *The Knight of the Burning Pestle*, by Beaumont and Fletcher (performed in 1607), help to limit the date and also indicate that at least one scene in *Macbeth* made a special impact on the Elizabethan audience. In *The Puritan* the reference is to a ghost in a "white sheet." In Beaumont and Fletcher's comedy, Jasper, pretending to be a ghost, enters with his face "mealed" (i.e., floured) and tells his enemy Venturewell,

> When thou art at thy table with thy friends,
> Merry in heart, and filled with swelling wine,
> I'll come in midst of all thy pride and mirth,
> Invisible to all men but thyself,
> And whisper such a sad tale in thine ear
> Shall make thee let the cup fall from thy hand,
> And stand as mute and pale as death itself.
>
> (V.i.23—9)

The two allusions point to a white-faced and perhaps white-robed ghost in *Macbeth*.

The earliest recorded performance of the play is that witnessed by Simon Forman, an astrologer, at the Globe Theatre on April 28, 1611. He wrote an account of what he saw (see Appendix D), but his memories of the play are confused with his memories of Holinshed, whose *Chronicles* he evidently knew, and in any case, his description tells us little about the way the play was staged.

Several sketches of the exterior of the Globe are to be seen in seventeenth-century views of London, but these early engravings provide conflicting evidence, and the building may have been circular or hexagonal. None of them shows the interior, but much can be learned from the surviving contract for the Fortune Theatre (built 1600), which specifies that its stage, galleries, and frame were to be "finished and done according to the manner and fashion of the said house called the Globe." From this contract, and from other evidence provided by plays and the comments of writers on theaters, it is well established that at the Globe a large platform stage extended into a yard in which the "groundlings" stood to watch plays. On either side of the stage were "gentlemen's rooms and twopenny rooms," as the Fortune contract stipulates, for the wealthier members of the audience. Those who could pay more than the groundlings, but not as much as the gentlemen, sat in one of the galleries which ran round the rest of the yard. The main acting area was the forestage,

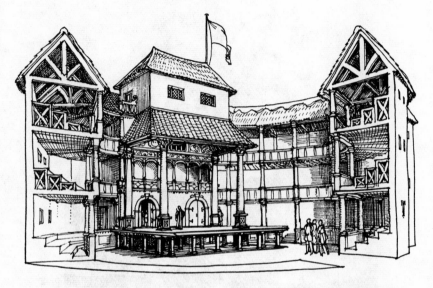

A reconstruction of a typical late Elizabethan playhouse, by C. Walter Hodges in his *The Globe Restored* (London: Ernest Benn, 1953). We do not know exactly how Shakespeare's Globe Theatre appeared to the actors and spectators, but a number of its known features are shown here. Among these are the arena where the "groundlings" stood to watch the play; the tiers of galleries where higher admission prices were charged; the large platform stage projecting into the arena, with a canopy supported on columns sheltering part of it; and the two doors, one on each side of the stage. No "inner stage" is shown, but curtains or a booth may have been erected between the doors to afford a location for certain kinds of scene, and the gallery over the stage was also probably used when needed.

The
High and mighty
Prince IAMES
KING of great
Britane Fraunce
and Ireland &c

Courtesy of the Royal Library, Windsor

An engraving of King James I on horseback, by Francis Delaram, undated but probably done in the earlier years of James's reign, perhaps about 1610. The Globe Theatre (center forefront) is here depicted as a circular structure. The other buildings displaying flags from a superstructure are presumably the Beargarden to the left and the Rose (pulled down in 1605) or the Swan Theatre. The large church between the horse's legs is St. Mary Overie's, and to the right the entrance to London Bridge is studded with poles bearing the heads of executed traitors (see *Macbeth*, Act V, scene viii, line 20 and note). The verses celebrating the king express the current mood of confidence in James I, a mood reflected in the compliment paid to James by Shakespeare in *Macbeth*; see the Introduction, pages xiv–xvii.

where the actor literally stood in the middle of his audience. Behind the open forestage was the tiring house (that is, the "attiring" house, or dressing rooms and backstage area), concealed from the audience by a two- or three-story frontage which probably looked to them like part of the interior of a large house. On the level of the stage, a curtained area, possibly a recess or a projecting tent, at the center of the tiring-house frontage was flanked by a door on each side. Above it was a balcony, perhaps with a window on either side; the stairs to this may have been visible. A "shadow" or "cover," supported on two pillars, projected over a good part of the open stage, and was roofed, making a kind of hut over the stage. This appears to have contained machinery for arranging descents from or ascents into the "heavens." On the platform itself were one or more trap doors providing for other kinds of ascent or descent.

Perhaps the main point to note about the tiring-house façade is that it could readily serve as either an exterior or interior setting. Some limited scenic effects, such as painted cloths, may have been used to indicate major changes of location. The open forestage provided an area for scenes not localized, or vaguely set "on a heath." Thus in *Macbeth* the transition from heath to castle, or from banquet hall to battlefield, did not demand changes in scenery. Indeed, the earliest printed texts of Shakespeare's plays give no scene locations at all. A change in costume (from, for instance, armor in Act I, scene iii, to nightgowns in Act II, scene iii), a stage effect (such as a little burnt resin to create a mist for the Witches), and properties (like the torch carried by Fleance in Act III, scene iii, to indicate nighttime, or the "leavy screens" brought on by the soldiers in Act V, scene vi) were enough to establish a setting. The furniture for the banquet in Act II, scene iv, was probably carried openly onto the stage and set up at the rear of the stage (where the ghost of Banquo could appear to best effect). Drums, flags, and a few weapons were all that was necessary to suggest the armies at the end.

Movements in the last act of the play are hard to interpret from the stage directions surviving in the earliest text, and editors disagree about the division of the action into scenes. This difficulty arises from the way in which plays were staged at the Globe. Scene divisions suggest breaks to us, but at the Globe these divisions were hardly, if at all, acknowledged. As one group of characters left the stage, another group swept on, perhaps through a different door if they wished to suggest a new location; and the flow of action was unhampered by elaborate changes of scenery. The act divisions may have meant something on the Elizabethan stage in the way of intervals, but even this is not certain. A sense of the flowing continuity of the action needs to be recaptured in performance if we are to appreciate the rhythm of the play, and is perhaps especially important for the gathering pace of the last scenes.

Apart from the performance seen by Simon Forman, nothing is known of the early stage history of the play. Its popularity is suggested by the influence it had on other playwrights who wrote plays involving witches and witchcraft. Perhaps the first was Ben Jonson in his *Masque of Queens* (1609), which may, along with *Macbeth*, have influenced Thomas Middleton in the writing of *The Witch* (date uncertain; perhaps about 1610). This play in turn affected the text of *Macbeth*, for two songs given in full in *The Witch* were added to Shakespeare's play (their first lines appear in the 1623 Folio text, III.v.32 and IV.i.43). Many critics think that all the dialogue involving Hecate (III.v and IV.i.39—43) was added at the same time, for Hecate appears in *The Witch*. The songs are associated with her, as is some elaborate stage business implied in her exit in Act III, scene v, where she may have floated into the heavens:

> . . . my little spirit, see,
> Sits in a foggy cloud, and stays for me.

These additions suggest an attempt to make the Witch scenes in *Macbeth* more varied and "pretty," and this softening process was continued when the theaters, closed in 1642, were reopened on the restoration of Charles II to the throne in 1660. *Macbeth*, one of the first plays to be revived, was now presented in a much debased version by Sir William D'Avenant. In his production the Witches flew off-stage on ropes or wires, their roles were expanded still further with more songs and dances, and they even appeared to Macduff and Lady Macduff. The result was very popular, and pleased Samuel Pepys, who praised it as "a most excellent play in all respects, especially in divertissement, though it be a deep tragedy" (*Diary*, January 7, 1667).

The "divertissements" provided by the Witches proved too good as popular fare to be sacrificed. When David Garrick restored the bulk of Shakespeare's text to the stage in 1744, he kept the opera-like entertainment of D'Avenant's Witch scenes, which, indeed, continued to affect productions of the play until late in the nineteenth century. For much of this period it remained customary, too, to omit the Porter scene and the scene between Lady Macduff and her son (IV.ii). In other words, the great actors of the period from Garrick to Henry Irving (who revived the play in 1875, 1888, and 1895) were all acting in versions more or less remote from Shakespeare's text and more or less lightened by musical Witches. It is perhaps remarkable that the force of the tragedy was felt at all.

The play was performed in the costume of the age until the late eighteenth century, when Charles Macklin introduced Scottish dress. At the Globe all the female parts had been played by boys or men, and one benefit of the new indoor, proscenium-arch theaters developed after the Restoration was the introduction of actresses to the stage—although the Witches continued to be played by men for a long time. Lady Macbeth became one of the great roles of some distinguished actresses, notably Mrs. Siddons, who played the role with beautiful majesty and a statuesque solemnity in the sleepwalking scene; she convinced two generations of theater-goers that hers was the only possible interpretation.

Nineteenth-century productions gradually restored more of Shakespeare's text and cut out the music and "divertissements," at the same time developing ever more elaborate scenery. Birnam Wood actually moved on stage, and Scottish castles were re-created in antiquarian splendor. All the great actors of the century played Macbeth and tried various interpretations of the role. Perhaps the most extreme was that of Henry Irving, who sacrificed nobility to make Macbeth a neurotic villain. An especially fine interpretation was Edwin Booth's; he managed to convey a sense both of the hero's physical strength and grandeur and of his inner discord and suffering.

The nineteenth-century theater throve on spectacle, and the mounting of elaborate scenes demanded long intervals as well as a sacrifice of parts of the text. In the present century a new understanding of the speed and simplicity of the staging at the Globe Theatre—fostered in England by the work and writings of directors like William Poel and Harley Granville-Barker—has restored to the stage a full text, swift succession of scenes, and the simplest of scenery. Again, most if not all leading actors of the day have attempted the part, and both John Gielgud and Laurence Olivier have given memorable interpretations. The play has been in the repertory of all the major Shakespeare Festival programs, from Stratford, England, to Stratford, Ontario. In Ontario heavy symbolism spoiled a production in which, for instance, poor Lady Macbeth entered carrying a milk churn—presumably containing milk of human kindness. Yet the actor who is allowed to play Shakespeare's text without such excess baggage can still reveal new nuances, new meanings, as, for example, Olivier did when, in 1955 at Stratford, England, he greeted the two Murderers in Act III, scene i, with beckoning fingers, drawing them to him on the phrase "Well then now" (III.i.74), until the three figures stood in a black-cloaked huddle, looking as sinister a group as the three Witches of Act I.

SHAKESPEARE'S TEXT AND THE PRESENT EDITION

Shakespeare was an actor and shareholder in the Globe Theatre. Like most other dramatists of the time, he took no thought for the publication of his plays, which became the property of his company, the King's Men. As long as a play retained an appeal in the theater, the actors had little or no interest in publishing it; the result was that many plays were not printed at all, and others appeared long after they were written. Thus *Macbeth* did not appear in print until the First Folio of Shakespeare's plays, gathered by his friends among the King's Men, was published in 1623, seven years after his death. The manuscript of the play had been in the possession of actors, who might have made various kinds of alteration in it for theatrical purposes, and when the play came into the printing house, it could have been further edited. These early acting manuscripts of Shakespeare's plays are lost, but the printed texts yield evidence of what lies behind them —and also evidence of alterations of Shakespeare's original version (see Appendix E).

The First Folio is so called because of its size; folio (Latin "by the leaf") consisted of sheets of the standard size (roughly 20 by 15 inches) folded once. This was the usual format for large books; for single plays, the most common size was quarto (Latin "in four"), in which the sheet was folded a second time. Thus in the Folio, when each sheet has been printed on both sides, it carries four pages of text, measuring 15 by 10 inches, whereas in a quarto each sheet yields eight pages of 10 by 7½ inches. Nineteen of Shakespeare's plays appeared in quarto editions before 1623, although *Macbeth* was first printed among the 36 plays in the Folio (F). This Folio was reprinted, with minor changes that have no authority, in 1632 (F2), 1664 (F3), and 1685 (F4).

The first "edition" in the modern sense was the work of Nicholas Rowe in 1709. He regularized the act and scene divisions, attempted a certain amount of emendation of unintelligible passages, and generally "tidied up" the text according to the taste of his time, which inclined toward a stricter metrical regularity than was usual a hundred years earlier. Subsequent editors followed Rowe's example, adding "corrections" to one another's work, until it became obvious in the present century that a fresh start must be made with the original texts.

The Folio text of *Macbeth* has act and scene divisions, but, like all other early editions, gives no scene locations. These were first added by eighteenth-century editors in accordance with an increasingly elaborate theatrical practice of representing scenes on the stage. Thus Rowe headed Act I, scene i, "An open heath," and Act I, scene ii, "A palace" (later editors modified this to "The palace at Forres," or "A camp near Forres"). Such headings, implying a change of representational scenery, were appropriate until this century, as conforming to general stage practice, but have no relevance to staging in Shakespeare's theater (see above). It is both false to the original text and misleading in relation to the nature of Shakespearean drama, in which the dialogue sets the scene, to give scene locations prominence. The only authentic indications of place and time are those found in the speeches of the characters. To help the reader, scene locations are discussed in the commentary of this edition, together with notation of time, especially in the first footnotes to individual scenes. It is important to remember, however, that scene flowed into scene, and the play could suggest at once continuous action and the passage of time (see notes to II.iv and III.vi).

This edition is based on the text of the Folio of 1623. Editors who have contributed much to our knowledge of the play are referred to in this volume in the commentary and elsewhere by name only, as Rowe, Pope, Theobald, Malone, etc. (see Appendix G). A full dated list of major editions may be found in recent volumes of the New Variorum Shakespeare, under the heading "Plan of the Work," or see E.K. Chambers, *William Shakespeare* (1930), I, 275–7. These lists do not include such important recent one-volume editions as those of G.L. Kittredge (1936), Peter Alexander (1951), and C.J. Sisson (1954). I have found certain modern editions very helpful, especially those of H.H. Furness, Jr. (New Variorum, revised 1903), E.K. Chambers (Warwick, 1873), J. Dover Wilson (New Cambridge, 1947), Kenneth Muir (New Arden, 1951, revised 1953), and Eugene Waith (Yale, 1954).

In this edition, the spelling and punctuation of the Folio text are modernized; in particular, I have reduced the heavy pointing of the Folio text to lighter modern punctuation, where this has proved possible without altering phrasing or emphasis. The First Folio's stage directions (abbreviated to "S.D." in the notes) have been preserved, but are expanded where necessary, and some new directions have been added to clarify the action for the reader. All material added is placed in square brackets. Quotations from other plays by Shakespeare, in the commentary and elsewhere, are cited from and use the lineation of the Tudor Shakespeare, edited by Peter Alexander. Abbreviations are listed in Appendix G.

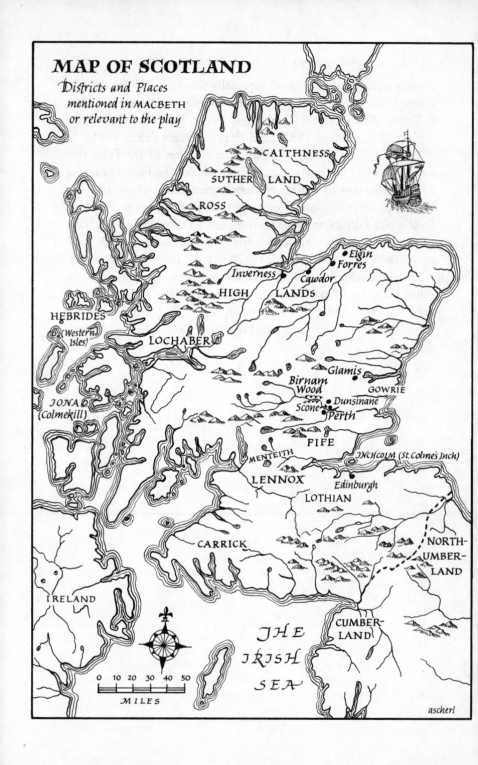

MAP OF SCOTLAND

Districts and Places
mentioned in MACBETH
or relevant to the play

CAITHNESS

SUTHER LAND

ROSS

Elgin
Forres

Inverness   Cawdor

HIGH   LANDS

HEBRIDES
(Western)
Isles)

LOCHABER

Glamis

Birnam
Wood   GOWRIE

JONA
(Colmekill)   Scone   Dunsinane
Perth

FIFE

INCHCOLM (St.Colme's Inch)
MENTEITH

LENNOX

Edinburgh

LOTHIAN

CARRICK   NORTH-
UMBER-
LAND

IRELAND

THE
CUMBER-
LAND

THE
IRISH

SEA

0 10 20 30 40 50
MILES

ascherl

CHARACTERS*

DUNCAN *King of Scotland.*

MALCOLM *Duncan's elder son and heir.*

DONALBAIN *Duncan's younger son.*

MACBETH *Duncan's cousin and general of his army.*

BANQUO *a nobleman sharing Macbeth's command as general of the army.*

MACDUFF ⎫
LENNOX ⎪
ROSS ⎬ *Scottish noblemen, called "thanes."*
MENTEITH ⎪
ANGUS ⎪
CAITHNESS ⎭

FLEANCE *son of Banquo.*

SIWARD *Earl of Northumberland, general of the English army.*

YOUNG SIWARD *his son.*

SEYTON *an officer attending on Macbeth.*

A Boy, son of Macduff.

A Scottish Doctor.

An English Doctor.

A Sergeant.

A Porter.

An Old Man.

LADY MACBETH *wife of Macbeth.*

LADY MACDUFF *wife of Macduff.*

Gentlewoman, attending on Lady Macbeth.

HECATE *goddess of witchcraft.*

Three Witches (so described on their entrance at Act I, scene i, but in the text called the "Weird Sisters").

The Ghost of Banquo

Apparitions (an armed head, a bloody child, and eight kings).

Lords, gentlemen, officers, soldiers, murderers, attendants, and messengers.

---

* There is no list of characters in the First Folio (F) of 1623; Nicholas Rowe first provided an incomplete list in his edition of 1709, and subsequent editors have modified and enlarged on this.

Time and Place

The events of the play range from the murder of Duncan, King of Scotland, which took place in 1046, to the death of Macbeth in 1057, and take place within the reign of Edward the Confessor, King of England 1042–66. The action is set in Scotland, with the exception of Act IV, scene iii, which is located at the English court.

The Tragedy of Macbeth

Act I, scene i: Thunder and lightning. Enter three Witches.

FIRST WITCH

When shall we three meet again?
In thunder, lightning, or in rain?

SECOND WITCH

When the hurly-burly's done,
When the battle's lost and won.

THIRD WITCH

5 That will be ere the set of sun.

FIRST WITCH

Where the place?

SECOND WITCH

Upon the heath.

THIRD WITCH

There to meet with Macbeth.

---

scene i The scene is not localized; it takes place in the open somewhere in Scotland. Thunder and lightning often heralded the appearance of supernatural beings on the Elizabethan stage, and here the
effects make a suitably startling opening.

S.D. *Enter . . .* Witches They are so called only in stage directions,
not in the text, where their nature is more ambiguous (see I.iii. 32
and note).

3. *hurly-burly* tumult.
6. *heath* the setting of I.iii (see line 77).

1

FIRST WITCH

I come, Graymalkin.

SECOND WITCH

Paddock calls.

THIRD WITCH

10   Anon!

ALL

Fair is foul, and foul is fair;
Hover through the fog and filthy air.

                                     Exeunt.

Scene ii: Alarum within. Enter KING [DUNCAN], MALCOLM, DONAL-
BAIN, LENNOX, *with attendants, meeting a bleeding* Captain.

DUNCAN

What bloody man is that? He can report,
As seemeth by his plight, of the revolt
The newest state.

---

8. *Graymalkin*   gray cat; "malkin," a diminutive of Matilda or Maud, was a name for a female demon especially associated with the cat.

9. *Paddock*   toad. Reginald Scot, *Discovery of Witchcraft*, I.iv, notes of witches: "Some say they can keep devils and spirits in the likeness of toads and cats."

9–10.   Assigned to "All" in F, but most editors now distribute the speeches; each Witch speaks to her own familiar spirit.

12. *Hover . . . fog*   Rowe thought that the Witches should fly off ("hover") here, but it is likely that at the Globe they slipped away into a "fog" made by burning resin.

Scene ii   The "battle" of I.i.4 is still going on, and the "alarum" (or call to arms) suggests that it is within earshot, but no specific locality is given. The verse in this scene is often metrically irregular (see, for example, lines 5, 7, 20, 37–43, 51, 66), reflecting perhaps the breathlessness of the dialogue, or dramatic pauses, as in the bleeding Captain's report.

MALCOLM

This is the sergeant,
Who, like a good and hardy soldier, fought
5 'Gainst my captivity—hail, brave friend!
Say to the King the knowledge of the broil
As thou didst leave it.

CAPTAIN

Doubtful it stood,
As two spent swimmers that do cling together
And choke their art. The merciless Macdonwald
10 (Worthy to be a rebel, for to that
The multiplying villanies of nature
Do swarm upon him) from the Western Isles
Of kerns and gallowglasses is supplied,
And Fortune, on his damnèd quarrel smiling,
15 Showed like a rebel's whore. But all's too weak,
For brave Macbeth (well he deserves that name),

---

3. *sergeant* pronounced as three syllables. He was of a much higher rank than a modern sergeant, having the standing of a knight (if he was a sergeant-at-arms and a personal attendant to the King) or of a squire, and could thus properly be called "Captain" in the stage directions.

6. *broil* battle.

9. *Macdonwald* Holinshed's "Macdowald" (see Appendix B, p. 161).

10. *to that* i.e., to that end.

12. *Western Isles* the Hebrides; the phrase is Holinshed's (see Appendix B, p. 161).

13. *kerns and gallowglasses* light- and heavy-armed Irish foot soldiers. According to Holinshed, Macdowald drew support both from the western isles, and from Ireland (see Appendix B, p. 161). F has "Gallowgrosses," a clear error.

14. *quarrel* This emendation of "quarry" (F) is supported by Holinshed's phrase "rebellious quarrel" (see Appendix B, p. 161).

15. *Showed . . . whore* i.e., appeared to have prostituted herself for Macdonwald. *all's* i.e., Macdonwald and Fortune together.

16. *name* i.e., the name "brave."

Disdaining Fortune, with his brandished steel,
Which smoked with bloody execution,
Like valour's minion carved out his passage,
20 Till he faced the slave;
Which ne'er shook hands, nor bade farewell to him,
Till he unseamed him from the nave to th' chops,
And fixed his head upon our battlements.

DUNCAN

O valiant cousin, worthy gentleman!

CAPTAIN

25 As whence the sun 'gins his reflection,
Shipwracking storms and direful thunders break,
So from that spring whence comfort seemed to come,
Discomfort swells. Mark, King of Scotland, mark:
No sooner justice had, with valour armed,
30 Compelled these skipping kerns to trust their heels,
But the Norweyan lord, surveying vantage,

---

18. *smoked* steamed.

19. *minion* favorite, or darling.

21. *Which* Some editors think a cut has been made after "slave," leaving this line hanging, but "Which" was often used for "who," and must refer to Macbeth (Abbott, 265). *shook hands* i.e., by way of taking leave of him.

22. *nave to th' chops* i.e., navel to the jaws.

24. *cousin* Duncan and Macbeth were grandsons of King Malcolm by his two daughters (see Appendix B, p. 161) and were therefore first cousins.

25. *whence . . . reflection* i.e., from where sunbeams are reflected or refracted through clouds; or possibly an allusion to storms associated with the spring (line 27) equinox.

26. *direful* dreadful.

27. *spring* The image is of a spring of water, but see line 25 and note.

30. *skipping* Being light-armed, they were easily able to run off.

31. *Norweyan lord* Sweno, King of Norway (see line 60). *surveying vantage* seeing his opportunity.

With furbished arms, and new supplies of men,
Began a fresh assault.

DUNCAN

Dismayed not this
Our captains, Macbeth and Banquo?

CAPTAIN

Yes,
35   As sparrows eagles, or the hare the lion.
If I say sooth, I must report they were
As cannons overcharged with double cracks,
So they
Doubly redoubled strokes upon the foe—
40   Except they meant to bathe in reeking wounds,
Or memorize another Golgotha,
I cannot tell—
But I am faint, my gashes cry for help.

DUNCAN

So well thy words become thee, as thy wounds;
45   They smack of honour both. Go, get him surgeons.

[*Exit* Captain, *escorted by attendants.*]
Enter ROSS *and* ANGUS.

Who comes here?

---

32. *furbished*   polished, therefore fresh. Rowe's correction of
"furbusht" (F).

36. *say sooth*   speak truth.

37. *cannons*   The Captain describes the battle in terms appropriate
to Shakespeare's age, not to the time of *Macbeth;* cannons were first
used in the fifteenth century. *cracks*   the noise of firing.

39–40. *foe—/Except*   The broken syntax and irregular verse in
this speech reflect the Captain's growing incoherence, and there is no
need to suppose, as some critics have, that the text is corrupt.

41. *Golgotha*   the "place of skulls" (Matthew 27:33) where Christ
was crucified.

MALCOLM

The worthy Thane of Ross.

LENNOX

What a haste looks through his eyes! So should he look
That seems to speak things strange.

ROSS

God save the King!

DUNCAN

Whence cam'st thou, worthy thane?

ROSS

From Fife, great King,
50 Where the Norweyan banners flout the sky,
And fan our people cold.
Norway himself, with terrible numbers,
Assisted by that most disloyal traitor,
The Thane of Cawdor, began a dismal conflict,
55 Till that Bellona's bridegroom, lapped in proof,
Confronted him with self-comparisons,
Point against point, rebellious arm 'gainst arm,

---

46. *Thane*   the chief of a clan, ranking as a baron, or nobleman.
48. *seems*   i.e., appears as if about to.
50. *flout*   insult. In reliving the action, Ross speaks for the moment
in the present tense.
51. *cold*   i.e., with fear.
54. *Thane of Cawdor*   Holinshed does not mention him in connection with this battle, but says that he was "condemned at Forres of
treason against the King committed" and his lands and titles bestowed
on Macbeth (see Appendix B, p. 163).
55. *Bellona's bridegroom*   i.e., Macbeth, here equated with Mars,
God of War. Bellona was, in fact, the sister of Mars in Roman myth.
lapped in proof   clad in impenetrable (proved or tested) armor.
56. *Confronted . . . self-comparisons*   faced him on equal terms.
The "comparison" becomes still closer later, when Macbeth, himself
"rebellious," is finally beheaded.

6

Curbing his lavish spirit; and to conclude,
The victory fell on us.

DUNCAN

Great happiness!

ROSS

60 That now Sweno,
The Norways' King, craves composition;
Nor would we deign him burial of his men
Till he disbursèd, at Saint Colme's Inch,
Ten thousand dollars to our general use.

DUNCAN

65 No more that Thane of Cawdor shall deceive
Our bosom interest: go, pronounce his present death,
And with his former title greet Macbeth.

ROSS

I'll see it done.

DUNCAN

What he hath lost, noble Macbeth hath won.

Exeunt.

---

58. *lavish* wild.
61. *composition* terms for submission.
63. *Saint Colme's Inch* the island of Saint Columba, in the Firth of Forth; the phrase is from Holinshed (see Appendix B, p. 162).
64. *dollars* English for the German *Thaler*, a silver coin first minted in the sixteenth century; an anachronism here.
65–7 See above, line 54 and note.
66. *bosom* dearest (as in "bosom friend").

7

Scene iii: Thunder. Enter three Witches.

FIRST WITCH

Where hast thou been, sister?

SECOND WITCH

Killing swine.

THIRD WITCH

Sister, where thou?

FIRST WITCH

A sailor's wife had chestnuts in her lap,
5 And munched, and munched, and munched. "Give me," quoth I;
"Aroint thee, witch!" the rump-fed ronyon cries.
Her husband's to Aleppo gone, master o' th' *Tiger*;
But in a sieve I'll thither sail,
And like a rat without a tail,
10 I'll do, I'll do, and I'll do.

Scene iii   The setting is a "blasted heath" (see line 77); the battle
is over, and Macbeth and Banquo are on their way to Forres, where
the King has apparently gone (see line 39 and note).

2. *Killing swine*   Witches showed their malevolence by killing pigs,
which were kept by peasant families to provide their main source of
meat.

6. *Aroint thee*   i.e., begone with a curse. The origin of the phrase
is not known; Shakespeare may have invented it. *rump-fed ronyon*
probably something like "fat-bottomed bitch." "Ronyon" is an un-
explained term of abuse, first used by Shakespeare (see *Merry Wives*
IV.ii.195).

7. *Aleppo . . . Tiger*   Aleppo is an inland city in northern Syria.
A voyage of 1583 to Tripoli, and thence overland to Aleppo, is described in Hakluyt's *Voyages*.

8. *sieve*   Witches were commonly supposed to sail about in sieves.

9. *rat . . . tail*   The popular belief was that although witches could
transform themselves into animals, some deficiency—like the lack
of a tail—would give them away.

SECOND WITCH

I'll give thee a wind.

FIRST WITCH

Th' art kind.

THIRD WITCH

And I another.

FIRST WITCH

I myself have all the other,
15 And the very ports they blow,
All the quarters that they know
I' th' shipman's card.
I'll drain him dry as hay;
Sleep shall neither night nor day
20 Hang upon his penthouse lid;
He shall live a man forbid.
Weary sev'n-nights, nine times nine,
Shall he dwindle, peak and pine;
Though his bark cannot be lost,
25 Yet it shall be tempest-tossed.
Look what I have.

SECOND WITCH

Show me, show me.

11–12. *wind . . . kind* The gift is a kind one because witches could sell the winds they commanded: "Witches for gold will sell a man a wind" (Thomas Nashe, *Summer's Last Will*, 1600; McKerrow, III.272).

14. *other* i.e., others; from the Middle English plural "oth(e)re."

15. *blow* blow upon; controlling the winds, she could prevent the ship from reaching a port by raising a contrary wind.

17. *card* i.e., compass; literally, the card marked with the thirty-two points of the compass.

20. *penthouse lid* i.e., eyelid, which slopes like a penthouse roof.

21. *forbid* accursed.

23. *peak and pine* droop and waste away.

9

FIRST WITCH

Here I have a pilot's thumb,
Wrecked as homeward he did come.

Drum within.

THIRD WITCH

30 A drum, a drum!
Macbeth doth come.

ALL

The Weird Sisters, hand in hand,
Posters of the sea and land,
Thus do go, about, about,
35 Thrice to thine, and thrice to mine,
And thrice again, to make up nine.
Peace! the charm's wound up.

Enter MACBETH *and* BANQUO.

MACBETH

So foul and fair a day I have not seen.

---

29. S.D. A drum is heard—as if the army is at hand—but Macbeth and Banquo enter alone, at line 37.

32. *Weird* Theobald's spelling "weyward" (F) indicates both that "Weird" should be pronounced as two syllables and that it has the sense "controlling men's fate," from the Old English "wyrd" meaning "fate" or, in the plural, "the Fates," or Parcae (the three goddesses supposed to control the course of human life). According to Holinshed, "the common opinion was that these women were either the Weird Sisters, that is (as ye would say), the goddesses of destiny, or else some nymphs or fairies" (see Appendix B, p. 163).

33. *Posters* i.e., swift travelers; the fastest way of travel in England was by post horse, galloping between short stages (see line 98 and note).

35–6. The Witches circle around nine times. Odd numbers, especially three and nine, traditionally figure in witchcraft, and in superstitious practices generally.

38. This line echoes I.i.11.

BANQUO

How far is't called to Forres?—What are these,

40 So withered, and so wild in their attire,

That look not like th' inhabitants o' th' earth,

And yet are on't? Live you, or are you aught

That man may question? You seem to understand me,

By each at once her choppy finger laying

45 Upon her skinny lips. You should be women,

And yet your beards forbid me to interpret

That you are so.

MACBETH

Speak if you can. What are you?

FIRST WITCH

All hail, Macbeth! hail to thee, Thane of Glamis!

SECOND WITCH

All hail, Macbeth! hail to thee, Thane of Cawdor!

THIRD WITCH

50 All hail, Macbeth! that shalt be King hereafter.

BANQUO

Good sir, why do you start, and seem to fear

Things that do sound so fair?

[*To the* Witches]   I' th' name of truth,

---

39. *Forres* a town in northern Scotland (see map, p. xxviii); Rowe's correction of "Soris" (F).

39—42. *What . . . on't* See Holinshed's "three women in strange wild apparel, resembling creatures of [an] elder world" (Appendix B, p. 163).

44. *choppy* chapped. The gesture was interpreted by A.C. Bradley in his *Shakespearean Tragedy* as a sign of refusal to speak to Banquo.

46. *beards* Witches were commonly supposed to have beards (see *Merry Wives* IV.ii.171).

48. *Glamis* See map, p. xxviii; a castle and village north of Dundee. The word is properly pronounced as one syllable, to rhyme with "alms," but Shakespeare treats it as two at I.v.13.

Are ye fantastical, or that indeed
Which outwardly ye show? My noble partner
55 You greet with present grace, and great prediction
Of noble having, and of royal hope,
That he seems rapt withal; to me you speak not.
If you can look into the seeds of time,
And say which grain will grow and which will not,
60 Speak then to me, who neither beg nor fear
Your favours, nor your hate.

FIRST WITCH

Hail!

SECOND WITCH

Hail!

THIRD WITCH

Hail!

FIRST WITCH

65 Lesser than Macbeth, and greater.

SECOND WITCH

Not so happy, yet much happier.

THIRD WITCH

Thou shalt get kings, though thou be none:
So all hail, Macbeth and Banquo!

FIRST WITCH

Banquo and Macbeth, all hail!

---

53. *fantastical* imaginary. According to Holinshed, Macbeth and
Banquo first thought that the Witches were "some vain fantastical illusion" (see Appendix B, p. 163).

55. *grace* honor.

56. *noble having* possession of nobility, i.e., as Thane of Cawdor.

66. *happy* fortunate (as "hap" meant "luck").

67. *get* beget.

12

MACBETH

70 Stay, you imperfect speakers, tell me more.
By Sinel's death I know I am Thane of Glamis,
But how of Cawdor? The Thane of Cawdor lives,
A prosperous gentleman. And to be King
Stands not within the prospect of belief,
75 No more than to be Cawdor. Say from whence
You owe this strange intelligence, or why
Upon this blasted heath you stop our way
With such prophetic greeting? Speak, I charge you!

                                        Witches *vanish*.

BANQUO

The earth hath bubbles, as the water has,
80 And these are of them. Whither are they vanished?

MACBETH

Into the air; and what seemed corporal melted
As breath into the wind. Would they had stayed!

BANQUO

Were such things here as we do speak about?
Or have we eaten on the insane root
85 That takes the reason prisoner?

---

71. *Sinel* Holinshed so names Macbeth's father.

72–3. *Thane . . . gentleman* Macbeth has just been fighting him (see I.ii.54–9); apparently Cawdor was taken prisoner (see I.ii.65–6), which Macbeth does not seem to know. The line may simply mean that Macbeth last saw the Thane of Cawdor alive and thriving (if not "prosperous" in the modern sense), hence his surprise.

76. *owe* have, own.

78. S.D. *vanish* again probably in mist made by burning resin.

79. *bubbles* deceptive shows (compare "the bubble reputation," *As You Like It* II.vii.152).

81. *corporal* corporeal, possessing a body.

84. *on* i.e., of; a common usage (Abbott, 181). *insane root* a root causing insanity; Shakespeare may have had one of several in mind, such as hemlock or henbane.

MACBETH

Your children shall be kings.

BANQUO

You shall be King.

MACBETH

And Thane of Cawdor too; went it not so?

BANQUO

To th' self-same tune and words. Who's here?

Enter ROSS *and* ANGUS.

ROSS

The King hath happily received, Macbeth,
90 The news of thy success; and when he reads
Thy personal venture in the rebels' fight,
His wonders and his praises do contend
Which should be thine or his. Silenced with that,
In viewing o'er the rest o' th' self-same day,
95 He finds thee in the stout Norweyan ranks
Nothing afeared of what thyself didst make,
Strange images of death. As thick as hail
Came post with post, and every one did bear
Thy praises in his kingdom's great defence
And poured them down before him.

---

91. *Thy . . . venture* referring to the fight with Macdonwald (see
I.ii.16ff).

92–3. *His . . . his* i.e., Duncan is torn between his own wonder at
the deed achieved and praise of Macbeth himself.

93. *that* "the mental conflict just described" (Wright).

95–7. *He . . . death.* referring to the fight with Sweno (see I.ii.52ff).

97–8. *hail / Came* Rowe's generally accepted correction of "Tale /
Can" (F); the phrase was in common use, and is listed as a proverb
by Tilley (H—11).

98. *post* swift messenger.

ANGUS

100   We are sent
To give thee from our royal master thanks,
Only to herald thee into his sight,
Not pay thee.

ROSS

And for an earnest of a greater honour,
105 He bade me, from him, call thee Thane of Cawdor;
In which addition, hail, most worthy thane,
For it is thine.

BANQUO

What, can the Devil speak true?

MACBETH

The Thane of Cawdor lives; why do you dress me
In borrowed robes?

ANGUS

               Who was the thane lives yet,
110 But under heavy judgment bears that life
Which he deserves to lose. Whether he was combined
With those of Norway, or did line the rebel
With hidden help and vantage, or that with both
He laboured in his country's wrack, I know not;
115 But treasons capital, confessed and proved,
Have overthrown him.

MACBETH

[*Aside*]   Glamis, and Thane of Cawdor:

---

104. *earnest* foretaste.
106. *addition* title, distinction.
112. *line* reinforce.
113. *vantage* profit, or benefit.
115—6. These lines foreshadow his own overthrow.

The greatest is behind. [*To* ROSS *and* ANGUS] Thanks for your
   pains.
[*To* BANQUO] Do you not hope your children shall be kings,
When those that gave the Thane of Cawdor to me
Promised no less to them?

BANQUO

120   That, trusted home,
Might yet enkindle you unto the crown,
Besides the Thane of Cawdor. But 'tis strange;
And oftentimes, to win us to our harm,
The instruments of darkness tell us truths,
125 Win us with honest trifles, to betray's
In deepest consequence.
   [*To* ROSS *and* ANGUS] Cousins, a word, I pray you.

MACBETH

[*Aside*]   Two truths are told
As happy prologues to the swelling act
Of the imperial theme. [*To the others*] I thank you, gentlemen.
130 [*Aside*] This supernatural soliciting
Cannot be ill, cannot be good. If ill,
Why hath it given me earnest of success,
Commencing in a truth? I am Thane of Cawdor.
If good, why do I yield to that suggestion
135 Whose horrid image doth unfix my hair

---

117. *behind*   i.e., still to come.

120. *trusted home*   thoroughly believed.

124. *darkness*   The image is Biblical in origin; see, for instance,
John 3:19, "light is come into the world, and men loved darkness
rather than light, because their deeds were evil."

125. *betray's*   betray us.

126. *In . . . consequence*   i.e., in matters of great importance.

128. *act*   acting out, performance (as *Henry VIII*, III.ii.183, ". . .
the honour of it / Does pay the act of it"); the use of "act" to signify
a division of a play was not yet current.

135. *image*   i.e., of himself murdering Duncan.

And make my seated heart knock at my ribs
Against the use of nature? Present fears
Are less than horrible imaginings.
My thought, whose murder yet is but fantastical,
140 Shakes so my single state of man,
That function is smothered in surmise,
And nothing is but what is not.

BANQUO

Look how our partner's rapt.

MACBETH

[*Aside*] If chance will have me King, why chance may crown me
Without my stir.

BANQUO

145   New honours come upon him
Like our strange garments, cleave not to their mould,
But with the aid of use.

MACBETH

[*Aside*]   Come what come may,
Time and the hour runs through the roughest day.

---

137. *Present fears* immediate objects of fear—contrasting with
"imaginings" of the future.

139. *fantastical* imaginary.

140. *single state* solitary, and hence unsupported, or weak, condition.

141–2. *function . . . not* I.e., normal activity (of mind and body)
is stifled by the speculations that overwhelm him, and his imaginings
alone seem real to him.

146. *strange garments* Perhaps Banquo and Macbeth on their way
to Forres to the King have discarded their battle armor for court attire, hence their garments feel "strange," or unfamiliar, but as an
image the phrase links with lines 108–9 above.

148. *runs* When two nouns formed one idea, it was common in
Elizabethan English to use a singular verb; many such false concords
are noted by Abbott (336).

BANQUO

Worthy Macbeth, we stay upon your leisure.

MACBETH

150 Give me your favour; my dull brain was wrought
With things forgotten. Kind gentlemen, your pains
Are registered where every day I turn
The leaf to read them. Let us toward the King.
[*To* BANQUO] Think upon what hath chanced, and at more time,
155 The interim having weighed it, let us speak
Our free hearts to each other.

BANQUO

                    Very gladly.

MACBETH

Till then, enough.—Come, friends.

                                        Exeunt.

Scene iv: Flourish. Enter KING [DUNCAN], MALCOLM, DONALBAIN,
LENNOX, *and attendants.*

DUNCAN

Is execution done on Cawdor? Or not
Those in commission yet returned?

---

150. *favour* pardon. *wrought* agitated.
152–3. *registered . . . them* i.e., as Dover Wilson notes, "within the book and volume of my brain" (*Hamlet* I.v.103).
155. *The . . . it* i.e., having thought about it in the interim.
156. *free hearts* unrestrained thoughts and feelings.
Scene iv Duncan's palace at Forres; no lapse of time is indicated, and though the scene has been regarded as taking place the day after scene iii, the questions with which this scene begins continue the impression of haste and of scenes flowing into one another.
1. *Or* Some editors emend to "Are," after F2.
2. *those in commission* those (i.e., Ross and Angus; see I.ii.66) entrusted with the duty.

MALCOLM
                     My liege,
They are not yet come back; but I have spoke
With one that saw him die, who did report
5   That very frankly he confessed his treasons,
Implored your highness' pardon, and set forth
A deep repentance. Nothing in his life
Became him like the leaving it. He died
As one that had been studied in his death,
10   To throw away the dearest thing he owed
As 'twere a careless trifle.

DUNCAN
                 There's no art
To find the mind's construction in the face:
He was a gentleman on whom I built
An absolute trust.—

       Enter MACBETH, BANQUO, ROSS, *and* ANGUS.
                 O worthiest cousin,
15   The sin of my ingratitude even now
Was heavy on me! Thou art so far before
That swiftest wing of recompense is slow
To overtake thee. Would thou hadst less deserved,
That the proportion both of thanks and payment
20   Might have been mine; only I have left to say,
More is thy due than more than all can pay.

---

6. *set forth*   displayed.
9. *studied . . . death*   skilled or practiced in the way to die.
10. *owed*   owned.
11–14. *There's . . . trust*   Ironically these lines can also apply to Macbeth, who enters just after they are spoken, or, as some actors have played the part, in time to overhear them.
12. *construction*   disposition.
19–20. *That . . . mine*   i.e., that I might have been able to reward you in proportion to your worth.

MACBETH

The service and the loyalty I owe,
In doing it, pays itself. Your highness' part
Is to receive our duties; and our duties
25 Are to your throne and state, children and servants,
Which do but what they should by doing everything
Safe toward your love and honour.

DUNCAN

           Welcome hither.
I have begun to plant thee, and will labour
To make thee full of growing. Noble Banquo,
30 That hast no less deserved, nor must be known
No less to have done so, let me enfold thee
And hold thee to my heart.

BANQUO

           There if I grow,
The harvest is your own.

DUNCAN

           My plenteous joys,
Wanton in fullness, seek to hide themselves
35 In drops of sorrow.—Sons, kinsmen, thanes,
And you whose places are the nearest, know

---

23. *In . . . itself* paraphrasing the proverb "Virtue is its own reward" (Tilley, V—81); "it" refers to "service" and "loyalty," as one
idea (see I.iii.148 and note).

25. *children and servants* Macbeth personifies the idea of "duties"
in an elaborate hyperbole.

27. *Safe . . . honour* i.e., to ensure your security in love and honor.

30—31. *nor . . . No* The double negative strengthens the force of
the statement (see Abbott, 406); we would say "and" now rather
than "nor."

34. *Wanton* irrepressible.

35. *kinsmen* Macbeth is first among them (see line 58).

36. *places* ranks, or offices.

We will establish our estate upon
Our eldest, Malcolm, whom we name hereafter
The Prince of Cumberland; which honour must
40 Not unaccompanied invest him only,
But signs of nobleness, like stars, shall shine
On all deservers. [*To* MACBETH] From hence to Inverness,
And bind us further to you.

MACBETH

The rest is labour, which is not used for you.
45 I'll be myself the harbinger, and make joyful
The hearing of my wife with your approach;
So humbly take my leave.

DUNCAN

My worthy Cawdor!

MACBETH

[*Aside*] The Prince of Cumberland—that is a step
On which I must fall down, or else o'er-leap,
50 For in my way it lies. Stars, hide your fires;
Let not light see my black and deep desires!

37–9. *establish . . . Cumberland* from Holinshed, who says, "He made the elder of them [his two sons], called Malcolm, Prince of Cumberland, as it were thereby to appoint him his successor in the kingdom" (see Appendix B, p. 164). The title was given to designate the heir to the throne in a succession that was not necessarily hereditary. Cumberland included a much larger area than the present English county, extending over a sizable stretch of what is now southern Scotland, and it owed allegiance to the Scottish crown.

42. *Inverness* "Envernes" in F. This is the first notice that Duncan is to visit Macbeth, and it comes so abruptly that some editors suspect corruption of the text here.

44. *which . . . you* which you are not accustomed to.

45. *harbinger* literally, an officer sent ahead to prepare lodgings for a royal visit.

The eye wink at the hand; yet let that be,
Which the eye fears, when it is done, to see.

Exit.

DUNCAN

True, worthy Banquo; he is full so valiant,
55   And in his commendations I am fed;
It is a banquet to me. Let's after him,
Whose care is gone before to bid us welcome.
It is a peerless kinsman.

Flourish. Exeunt.

Scene v: Enter LADY MACBETH, *reading a letter.*

LADY MACBETH

"They met me in the day of success; and I have learned by the
perfect'st report, they have more in them than mortal knowledge. When I burned in desire to question them further, they
made themselves air, into which they vanished. Whiles I
5   stood rapt in the wonder of it, came missives from the King,
who all-hailed me Thane of Cawdor; by which title, before,
these Weird Sisters saluted me, and referred me to the coming
on of time, with 'Hail, King that shalt be!' This have I thought

---

52. *wink . . . hand*   overlook, connive at what the hand does. *be*
i.e., be done.

54. During Macbeth's soliloquy, Banquo has apparently praised
him to Duncan, who replies in this line.

58. *kinsman*   Macbeth was Duncan's cousin (see I.ii.24 and note).

Scene v   The action moves now to Macbeth's castle in Inverness,
following on from I.iv.42.

2. *perfect'st report*   most reliable information.

4. *made . . . air*   See I.iii.80–82.

5–6. *King . . . Cawdor*   In fact it was the Witches who "all-hailed"
him, at I.iii.49.

good to deliver thee (my dearest partner of greatness) that
10 thou might'st not lose the dues of rejoicing by being ignorant
of what greatness is promised thee. Lay it to thy heart, and
farewell."
Glamis thou art, and Cawdor, and shalt be
What thou art promised. Yet do I fear thy nature;
15 It is too full o' th' milk of human kindness
To catch the nearest way. Thou wouldst be great;
Art not without ambition, but without
The illness should attend it. What thou wouldst highly,
That wouldst thou holily; wouldst not play false,
20 And yet wouldst wrongly win. Thou'dst have, great Glamis,
That which cries, "Thus must thou do," if thou have it;
And that which rather thou dost fear to do,
Than wishest should be undone. Hie thee hither,
That I may pour my spirits in thine ear,
25 And chastise with the valour of my tongue
All that impedes thee from the golden round,

---

9. *deliver* tell.

14. *fear* mistrust.

15. *milk of human kindness* The phrase has passed into common usage. Lady Macbeth implies that Macbeth has too much gentleness of disposition (compare "milky gentleness," *Lear* I.iv.342), and comments adversely on what to her is weakness; but overtones in the phrase like "humane," "kinship" (a possible meaning of "kindness"), and "humankind" suggest that what she criticizes is proper to all human beings, and natural to man.

18. *illness* wickedness. The word came to be used in its familiar sense of "sickness" only at the end of the seventeenth century.

20–23. *Thou'dst . . . undone* There are no quotation marks in F, and editors have disagreed on where the end quote should come, often placing it after "undone" (line 23). But "Thou'dst have" (line 20) seems to have two objects: "That" in line 21 (i.e., the crown which cries murder is necessary) and "that" in line 22 (i.e., the murder itself).

25. *chastise* accented on the first syllable, as is usual in Shakespeare.

Which Fate and metaphysical aid doth seem
To have thee crowned withal.

            Enter [a] Messenger.

                    What is your tidings?

MESSENGER

The King comes here tonight.

LADY MACBETH

                  Thou'rt mad to say it.

30 Is not thy master with him?—who, wer't so,
Would have informed for preparation.

MESSENGER

So please you, it is true; our thane is coming.
One of my fellows had the speed of him,
Who, almost dead for breath, had scarcely more
Than would make up his message.

LADY MACBETH

35   Give him tending,
He brings great news.

                         Exit Messenger.

            The raven himself is hoarse
That croaks the fatal entrance of Duncan

---

27. *metaphysical* supernatural. *doth* The two nouns form one idea, and the verb is singular (see I.iii.148 and note).

27–8. *Which . . . withal* equivalent to "With which."

28. *tidings* used indiscriminately by Shakespeare with a singular or plural verb.

31. *informed* sent word. *preparation* pronounced as five syllables.

33. *had the speed of* outdistanced.

36. *raven* a bird of ill-omen; see *Caesar* V.i.84–9, and *Othello* IV.i.20, "As doth the raven o'er the infected house / Boding to all."

Under my battlements. Come, you spirits
That tend on mortal thoughts, unsex me here,
40 And fill me from the crown to the toe, top-full
Of direst cruelty! Make thick my blood,
Stop up th' access and passage to remorse,
That no compunctious visitings of nature
Shake my fell purpose, nor keep peace between
45 Th' effect and it! Come to my woman's breasts,
And take my milk for gall, you murd'ring ministers,
Wherever in your sightless substances
You wait on nature's mischief! Come, thick night,
And pall thee in the dunnest smoke of Hell,
50 That my keen knife see not the wound it makes,

---

38. *my* a significant pronoun, seized on by many actresses to register Lady Macbeth's dominance here. *Come . . . spirits* The line is a syllable short, suggesting a pause before this terrible invocation of hellish spirits.

39. *mortal* murderous; compare III.iv.80.

41. *make . . . blood* i.e., so that no pity will flow from her heart to disturb the resolution of her mind.

42. *remorse* pity.

43. *compunctious* remorseful; a word apparently coined by Shakespeare.

44–5. *keep . . . it* i.e., intervene to make peace between my cruel purpose and its fulfilment, and so restrain me.

45. *it* F3; "hit" (F) is a plain error.

46. *take . . . gall* i.e., replace the milk with gall. *ministers* attendant spirits, as at *Tempest* III.iii.89.

47. *sightless* invisible.

48. *nature's mischief* Perhaps this refers to the evil-doing that violates the natural order; but it could also mean the evil-doing which springs out of (human) nature and to which man, in his fallen condition, is prone.

49. *pall thee* cover thee (i.e., Duncan) as with a pall, a cloth spread over a coffin. *dunnest* darkest.

50. *my* Some critics have argued from this that Lady Macbeth intends here to murder Duncan herself; see lines 65–6 and line 71 in this scene, and II.ii.12–13.

Nor Heaven peep through the blanket of the dark
To cry, "Hold, hold!"

Enter MACBETH.

Great Glamis! Worthy Cawdor!
Greater than both, by the all-hail hereafter!
Thy letters have transported me beyond
55 This ignorant present, and I feel now
The future in the instant.

MACBETH

My dearest love,
Duncan comes here tonight.

LADY MACBETH

And when goes hence?

MACBETH

Tomorrow, as he purposes.

LADY MACBETH

O never
Shall sun that morrow see!
60 Your face, my thane, is as a book, where men
May read strange matters: to beguile the time,
Look like the time, bear welcome in your eye,
Your hand, your tongue; look like the innocent flower,
But be the serpent under't. He that's coming

---

51. *blanket* suggesting a world asleep and Duncan in bed.

53. *hereafter* See line 8 above; she thinks of him as King in the future.

55. *ignorant* i.e., not knowing what is to come.

61–2. *to . . . time* i.e., to deceive society, behave as the world does. For "time" in this sense of society at large, see also I.vii.82.

63–4. *look . . . under't* a proverbial idea, deriving from Virgil's *Eclogues* (*latet anguis in herba*—"a serpent hides in the grass"), which is illustrated in Geoffrey Whitney's *Choice of Emblems* (1586) by a picture of a serpent and a strawberry plant, with verses warning

65 Must be provided for; and you shall put
    This night's great business into my dispatch,
    Which shall to all our nights and days to come
    Give solely sovereign sway and masterdom.

                    MACBETH
    We will speak further.

                    LADY MACBETH
                        Only look up clear;
70 To alter favour ever is to fear.
    Leave all the rest to me.

                                        Exeunt.

    Scene vi: Oboes and torches. Enter KING [DUNCAN], MALCOLM,
    DONALBAIN, BANQUO, LENNOX, MACDUFF, ROSS, ANGUS, *and*
    attendants.

                    DUNCAN
    This castle hath a pleasant seat; the air
    Nimbly and sweetly recommends itself
    Unto our gentle senses.

---

men to "Suspect the heart whose face doth fawn and smile"; the
current phrase is "snake in the grass" (Tilley, S—585).
66. *dispatch*   management.
68. *solely*   i.e., to us alone.
69. *clear*   cheerfully.
70. *favour*   facial expression.
Scene vi   The verse creates imaginatively the entrance to Macbeth's
castle, which was sufficiently suggested at the Globe by the neutral
tiring-house façade (see Introduction, p. xxi).
S.D. The entry suggests a stately royal progress.
1. *seat*   situation.
2. *nimbly*   briskly.
3. *gentle senses*   i.e., senses made gentle, soothed by the breeze.
This form of construction (proleptic) is fairly common in Shakespeare
(see III.iv.75).

27

BANQUO

This guest of summer,
The temple-haunting martlet, does approve,
5 By his loved masonry, that the heaven's breath
Smells wooingly here. No jutty, frieze,
Buttress, nor coign of vantage, but this bird
Hath made his pendant bed and procreant cradle;
Where they most breed and haunt, I have observed
The air is delicate.

Enter LADY [MACBETH].

DUNCAN

10   See, see, our honoured hostess!
The love that follows us sometime is our trouble,
Which still we thank as love. Herein I teach you
How you shall bid God 'ield us for your pains,
And thank us for your trouble.

---

4. *martlet*   house martin; Rowe's emendation of "Barlet" (F).

5. *masonry*   Pope offered this correction of "Mansonry" (F), which
fits the martlet's nest ("pendant bed and procreant cradle") in line 8,
but Theobald's "Mansionry" has been preferred by most editors, who
cannot agree on its meaning ("building of mansions" or "fondness for
this mansion"); the coinage is more likely to be Theobald's than
Shakespeare's.

6. *jutty*   projection (a variant of "jetty").

7. *coign of vantage*   favorable corner. "Coign" is a variant of
"quoin," from the French *coin*, meaning "corner."

9. *most*   Rowe's emendation of "must" (F).

10. *delicate*   mild and pleasant.

11–14. A ceremonious way of saying that his visit is made out of
love of his hostess and host; the sense is roughly: The attentions of
those who love me ("us" is the royal plural) are sometimes a nuisance,
but yet I am grateful to them; in this way I teach you how to pray
("bid") God to reward (" 'ield," i.e., yield) me for the trouble you take,
and thank me for being a nuisance to you.

LADY MACBETH

All our service
15 In every point twice done, and then done double,
Were poor and single business to contend
Against those honours deep and broad wherewith
Your majesty loads our house: for those of old,
And the late dignities heaped up to them,
We rest your hermits.

DUNCAN

20   Where's the Thane of Cawdor?
We coursed him at the heels, and had a purpose
To be his purveyor; but he rides well,
And his great love, sharp as his spur, hath holp him
To his home before us. Fair and noble hostess,
We are your guest tonight.

LADY MACBETH

25   Your servants ever
Have theirs, themselves, and what is theirs, in compt,
To make their audit at your highness' pleasure,
Still to return your own.

DUNCAN

Give me your hand:

---

16. *single* feeble; compare I.iii.140.

16–17. *contend / Against* compete with.

20. *rest your hermits* i.e., shall go on saying prayers for you;
"hermits" here means "beadsmen," as at *Titus Andronicus* III.ii.41.

22. *purveyor* an officer sent in advance to provide supplies against
the arrival of a king or great lord. The word is accented on the first
syllable.

23. *holp* The early strong inflection only gradually gave way to
the modern "helped"; Shakespeare uses both forms.

26. *theirs, in compt* i.e., their servants, themselves, and their
property, in reckoning (or in trust, as we might now say); "compt"
is a variant of "count" (modern "account").

Conduct me to mine host; we love him highly,
30 And shall continue our graces towards him.
By your leave, hostess.

                          Exeunt.

*Scene vii: Oboes. Torches. Enter a Sewer, and divers servants
with dishes and service [who pass] over the stage. Then enter*
MACBETH.

MACBETH

If it were done when 'tis done, then 'twere well
It were done quickly. If th' assassination
Could trammel up the consequence, and catch
With his surcease, success; that but this blow
5 Might be the be-all and the end-all—here,

---

31. *By your leave* said as apology for taking a liberty; it might
refer merely to his taking her hand, or perhaps to a further liberty,
such as kissing her hand or even her cheek.
  Scene vii within the castle some hours later; the torches indicate
to the audience that it is evening, for there was no lighting at the
Globe Theatre and the performances took place in daylight.
  S.D. *Oboes* The music is presumably heard but not seen, and
again, as in I.vi, suggests a ceremonious occasion, here a state banquet.
Sewer "Attendants who superintended the arrangement of the table,
the seating of guests, and the tasting and serving of the dishes" (*OED*);
derived from the French *asseoir* (to sit or seat).
  1. *If . . . 'tis done* i.e., if it were at an end, altogether finished, at
the moment the deed is done.
  2–7. *If . . . come* i.e., if the murder could have no consequences
(literally, if it could catch them in a trammel, or net) and could seize
success with Duncan's death; if only this blow could be in itself sufficient and in itself complete, then here, at this point in the flow of
time, I would take a chance on the life to come (and, he implies, do the
deed). The passage is complicated, for "his surcease" could refer to
the completion of the deed, as well as to the death of Duncan, and "the
life to come" suggests both Macbeth's life on this earth and his eternal
life (see III.i.67–8). No paraphrase can do justice to it.

But here, upon this bank and shoal of time,
We'd jump the life to come. But in these cases,
We still have judgment here, that we but teach
Bloody instructions, which being taught return
10   To plague th' inventor. This even-handed justice
Commends th' ingredients of our poisoned chalice
To our own lips. He's here in double trust:
First, as I am his kinsman and his subject,
Strong both against the deed; then, as his host,
15   Who should against his murderer shut the door,
Not bear the knife myself. Besides, this Duncan
Hath borne his faculties so meek, hath been
So clear in his great office, that his virtues
Will plead like angels, trumpet-tongued, against
20   The deep damnation of his taking-off;
And pity, like a naked, new-born babe
Striding the blast, or Heaven's cherubins, horsed

---

6. *shoal* "Schoole" (F) was a possible spelling of "shoal," Theobald's generally accepted reading, which images an island in the sea of time—as if Macbeth wishes the flow of time to stop with Duncan's death—and suggests that this life is a "narrow bank in the ocean of eternity" (Johnson). The alternative interpretation is to take "bank" as a bench in a school.

7. *jump* risk.

8–12. *have . . . lips* i.e., are sentenced in this life, for in teaching others to murder, we make ourselves liable to the same end.

10. *even-handed* impartial.

11. *ingredients* "ingredience" (F) was a common form of the word, singular or plural, but it arose as a misspelling of "ingredients."

17. *borne . . . meek* exercised his powers so mildly.

18. *clear* blameless.

20. *taking-off* murder; compare III.i.105.

22. *Striding* bestriding. *blast* suggested probably by "trumpet-tongued" (line 19), and in turn suggesting a storm of indignation.

22–3. *Heaven's . . . air* Compare Psalms 18:10 (*Book of Common Prayer*): "He rode upon the Cherubims and did fly; he came flying upon the wings of the wind"; F has "Cherubin," and Shakespeare's usual plural form is "cherubins," adopted here. *OED* first records the

Upon the sightless couriers of the air,
Shall blow the horrid deed in every eye,
25   That tears shall drown the wind. I have no spur
To prick the sides of my intent, but only
Vaulting ambition, which o'er-leaps itself,
And falls on th' other.

Enter LADY [MACBETH].
How now? What news?

LADY MACBETH

He has almost supped. Why have you left the chamber?

MACBETH

Hath he asked for me?

LADY MACBETH

30   Know you not he has?

MACBETH

We will proceed no further in this business.
He hath honoured me of late, and I have bought
Golden opinions from all sorts of people,
Which would be worn now in their newest gloss,
Not cast aside so soon.

LADY MACBETH

35   Was the hope drunk

---

correct Hebrew plural, "cherubim," in 1605, and Shakespeare is not
likely to have known it.

23. *sightless couriers*   invisible runners, i.e., the winds.

25–8. *I . . . other*   i.e., ambition alone spurs on my design, and
ambition, vaulting into the saddle (or royal seat), leaps too far, and
falls on the other side (into disgrace or ruin). The image begins with
Macbeth as the rider of a horse that is "intent," or ambition; then
"ambition" becomes the rider, and the seat aimed at is the royal
throne. The shifting metaphor is compressed and confused, reflecting
Macbeth's state of mind.

34. *would*   should.

Wherein you dressed yourself? Hath it slept since?
And wakes it now to look so green and pale
At what it did so freely? From this time,
Such I account thy love. Art thou afeard
40   To be the same in thine own act and valour
As thou art in desire? Wouldst thou have that
Which thou esteem'st the ornament of life,
And live a coward in thine own esteem,
Letting "I dare not" wait upon "I would,"
Like the poor cat i' th' adage?

MACBETH

45   Prithee, peace.
I dare do all that may become a man;
Who dares do more is none.

LADY MACBETH

                            What beast was't then
That made you break this enterprise to me?
When you durst do it, then you were a man;
50   And to be more than what you were, you would

---

37. *green and pale* as if with a hangover, but "green and pale" is
also associated with fear.

39. *Such* i.e., as worth only contempt.

41. *that* i.e., the crown.

45. *Like . . . adage* alluding to the proverb "The cat would eat fish
but she will not wet her feet" (Tilley, C—144).

47. *do* Rowe's generally accepted correction of "no" (F) is supported by the lines following. *is none* i.e., must be other than human;
devilish, as Macbeth seems to mean, or beastly, as Lady Macbeth
chooses to interpret it.

48. *break* make known. Since there is no scene shown in which
Macbeth "breaks this enterprise" to Lady Macbeth, some critics think
that this line is evidence for an original longer version of the play (see
Dover Wilson, pp. xxxiv—xxxviii). It is better taken as an instance of
suggestive compression in the dialogue; see also the discussion in
A.C. Bradley's *Shakespearean Tragedy*, pp. 480—84.

Be so much more the man. Nor time, nor place
Did then adhere, and yet you would make both;
They have made themselves, and that their fitness now
Does unmake you. I have given suck, and know
55 How tender 'tis to love the babe that milks me;
I would, while it was smiling in my face,
Have plucked my nipple from his boneless gums
And dashed the brains out, had I so sworn
As you have done to this.

MACBETH

If we should fail?

LADY MACBETH

60 We fail?
But screw your courage to the sticking-place,
And we'll not fail. When Duncan is asleep
(Whereto the rather shall his day's hard journey
Soundly invite him), his two chamberlains
65 Will I with wine and wassail so convince,
That memory, the warder of the brain,
Shall be a fume, and the receipt of reason
A limbec only; when in swinish sleep

---

52. *adhere* link together (i.e., as appropriate for murder).

54. *unmake* unnerve.

54–9. *I . . . this* Neither Holinshed nor Shakespeare directly speaks of Lady Macbeth as having a child. See also I.v.45–6.

61. *But . . . sticking-place* i.e., only set your heart firmly on the deed. The image may be derived from "the screwing-up of the peg" of a stringed instrument until it is tightly fixed and the string given tension (*OED*).

64. *chamberlains* attendants in the King's bedchamber.

65. *wine . . . convince* i.e., overcome with strong drink; "convince" is used in its original Latin sense, from *vincere*, to vanquish.

66–8. *memory . . . only* The head was divided by early physiologists into three compartments, and in the lowest, at the base of the skull, memory was located, placed like a guard or watchman. Strong

Their drenchèd natures lie, as in a death,
70 What cannot you and I perform upon
Th' unguarded Duncan? What not put upon
His spongy officers, who shall bear the guilt
Of our great quell?

MACBETH

Bring forth men-children only!
For thy undaunted mettle should compose
75 Nothing but males. Will it not be received,
When we have marked with blood those sleepy two
Of his own chamber, and used their very daggers,
That they have done't?

LADY MACBETH

Who dares receive it other,
As we shall make our griefs and clamour roar
Upon his death?

MACBETH

80   I am settled, and bend up
Each corporal agent to this terrible feat.

---

drink could turn the memory to vapor, and so make the container
("receipt") of reason, the brain itself, merely an alembic ("limbec"),
or a still, full of a confused alcoholic haze.

69. *drenchèd* drowned.

72. *spongy* i.e., soaked with drink.

73. *quell* murder; in origin apparently the same word as "kill."

74. *mettle* a variant of "metal," meaning the stuff composing the
human personality, as at *Lear* I.i.68, "I am made of that self metal as
my sister."

75. *received* accepted as true.

78. *other* otherwise.

80–81. *bend . . . agent* brace every faculty of the body; "bend up"
(from bringing a bow into tension) in this usage was probably a dead
metaphor by this time.

Away, and mock the time with fairest show;
False face must hide what the false heart doth know.

                                              Exeunt.

Act II, scene i: Enter BANQUO *and* FLEANCE, *with a torch before him.*

BANQUO

How goes the night, boy?

FLEANCE

The moon is down; I have not heard the clock.

BANQUO

And she goes down at twelve.

FLEANCE

                    I take't, 'tis later, sir.

BANQUO

Hold, take my sword.—There's husbandry in Heaven,
5   Their candles are all out.—Take thee that too.—
A heavy summons lies like lead upon me,

82–3. See I.v.61–2 and note. The line varies the common proverb "False face, foul heart" (Tilley, F–3).

scene i the castle, later at night. The tiring-house façade at the Globe could suggest an exterior or interior wall (see Introduction, p. xxi); and the action in these scenes moves in and around the castle. Dover Wilson thought of this scene as taking place in an inner courtyard, with Fleance looking up at the open sky (see line 2) rather than out of a window.

S.D. *torch before him* i.e., possibly a servant carrying a torch, for Fleance is loaded down with other props at lines 4–5; but the more specific stage direction at line 9 has led editors and directors to give Fleance the torch here.

4. *husbandry* thrift.

5. *that* probably his belt and hanger, or his shield.

6. *summons* i.e., to sleep.

And yet I would not sleep. Merciful Powers,
Restrain in me the cursèd thoughts that nature
Gives way to in repose!—Give me my sword.

Enter MACBETH, *and a servant with a torch.*

10 Who's there?

MACBETH

A friend.

BANQUO

What, sir, not yet at rest? The King's abed;
He hath been in unusual pleasure, and
Sent forth great largess to your offices.
15 This diamond he greets your wife withal
By the name of most kind hostess, and shut up
In measureless content.

MACBETH

      Being unprepared,
Our will became the servant to defect,
Which else should free have wrought.

BANQUO

            All's well.
20 I dreamed last night of the three Weird Sisters;
To you they have showed some truth.

---

7. *Powers* W.C. Curry, *Shakespeare's Philosophical Patterns*, p. 81,
describes them as the order of angels especially concerned with restraining demons (Milton lists the orders in *Paradise Lost* V.601, as
"Thrones, Dominations, Princedoms, Virtues, Powers"), but a more
general reference was perhaps intended.

14. *largess . . . offices* gifts of money to the servants' quarters.

16. *shut up* i.e., retired to his room.

17–19. *Being . . . wrought* a labored apology, to this effect: As
we were unprepared, our desire to be generous in our hospitality to
the King was hampered; otherwise we should have done much more.

MACBETH

I think not of them;
Yet when we can entreat an hour to serve,
We would spend it in some words upon that business,
If you would grant the time.

BANQUO

At your kind'st leisure.

MACBETH

25 If you shall cleave to my consent, when 'tis,
It shall make honour for you.

BANQUO

So I lose none
In seeking to augment it, but still keep
My bosom franchised, and allegiance clear,
I shall be counselled.

MACBETH

Good repose the while!

BANQUO

30 Thanks, sir; the like to you.

Exeunt BANQUO [*and* FLEANCE].

MACBETH

Go, bid thy mistress, when my drink is ready,

---

22. *we* Macbeth falls into the royal plural before he has the throne.

25. *cleave . . . 'tis* an ambiguous feeler, meaning both "adhere to my party when the time comes (of Duncan's death)" and "follow my advice (when we have our talk)."

28. *bosom . . . clear* thoughts free (from guilt), and allegiance innocent. Banquo is warning Macbeth that he will have no share in foul play.

31–2. *bid . . . bell* apparently a prearranged signal, to tell him all is quiet (see lines 62–3 of this scene). The drink would be a "posset" or nightcap (see II.ii.6 and note).

She strike upon the bell. Get thee to bed.

Exit [*servant*].

Is this a dagger which I see before me,
The handle toward my hand? Come, let me clutch thee:—
35 I have thee not, and yet I see thee still.
Art thou not, fatal vision, sensible
To feeling as to sight? Or art thou but
A dagger of the mind, a false creation
Proceeding from the heat-oppressèd brain?
40 I see thee yet, in form as palpable
As this which now I draw.
Thou marshall'st me the way that I was going,
And such an instrument I was to use.—
Mine eyes are made the fools o' th' other senses,
45 Or else worth all the rest.—I see thee still;
And on thy blade and dudgeon, gouts of blood,
Which was not so before.—There's no such thing;
It is the bloody business which informs
Thus to mine eyes.—Now o'er the one half-world
50 Nature seems dead, and wicked dreams abuse
The curtained sleep. Witchcraft celebrates
Pale Hecate's offerings; and withered murder,

---

36. *sensible*   perceptible by the senses (the word's original meaning).

39. *heat-oppressèd*   fevered (Dover Wilson).

42. *marshall'st . . . going*   i.e., the dagger seems to move, and to lead Macbeth toward Duncan's room.

44–5. *Mine . . . rest*   i.e., either my eyes are deceived by the other senses (which do not apprehend the dagger), or else they report the truth and are worth all the rest (which, in that case, are giving false information).

46. *dudgeon*   wooden handle. *gouts*   drops (French *goutte*).

48. *informs*   takes visible shape.

51. The line is a syllable short, probably to provide a pause after "sleep." D'Avenant's version has "now witchcraft . . ."

52. *Hecate's offerings*   offerings made to Hecate, a goddess who

Alarumed by his sentinel, the wolf,
Whose howl's his watch, thus with his stealthy pace,
55 With Tarquin's ravishing strides, towards his design
Moves like a ghost.—Thou sure and firm-set Earth,
Hear not my steps, which way they walk, for fear
Thy very stones prate of my whereabout,
And take the present horror from the time,
60 Which now suits with it.—Whiles I threat, he lives:
Words to the heat of deeds too cold breath gives.

A bell rings.

I go, and it is done; the bell invites me.
Hear it not, Duncan, for it is a knell
That summons thee to Heaven, or to Hell.

Exit.

Scene ii: Enter LADY [MACBETH].

LADY MACBETH

That which hath made them drunk hath made me bold;

---

presided over witchcraft and was associated with the moon (compare
III.ii.41).

53. *Alarumed*   roused to action.

54. *watch*   signal.

55. *Tarquin's . . . strides*   alluding to Tarquin's rape of Lucretia,
wife of Collatinus; see Shakespeare's *Rape of Lucrece*, line 365, "Into
the chamber wickedly he stalks." F has "sides," emended by Pope to
"strides," and generally accepted since.

56. *sure*   Pope's emendation of "soure" (F); Dover Wilson cites
Psalms 93:2.

59–60. *take . . . time*   Macbeth relishes his own sense of horror,
and to disturb this would be to shatter his resolution.

61. *gives*   See note to I.iii.148.

62. *bell*   See V.i.28 and note.

Scene ii   There is no break in the action. Lady Macbeth enters as
Macbeth leaves. In many productions Macbeth climbs a flight of

What hath quenched them hath given me fire.—Hark! Peace,
It was the owl that shrieked, the fatal bellman,
Which gives the stern'st good night. He is about it,
5 The doors are open; and the surfeited grooms
Do mock their charge with snores. I have drugged their possets,
That death and nature do contend about them
Whether they live or die.

Enter MACBETH.

MACBETH

         Who's there? What ho?

LADY MACBETH

Alack! I am afraid they have awaked,
10 And 'tis not done; th' attempt and not the deed
Confounds us: hark!—I laid their daggers ready,
He could not miss 'em. Had he not resembled
My father as he slept, I had done't.—My husband?

---

stairs, as though to a bedchamber, to make his exit; a swift bound up
the last steps can effectively register the impact of his decision. However, there is no evidence to show how this was staged at the Globe.

    1. *That*   i.e., wine (see I.vii.65).

    3. *owl . . . bellman*   One of the tasks of a bellman, or town crier,
was to announce deaths, and the owl was known as a bird of ill omen,
for its "death-boding cries" (*Rape of Lucrece*, line 165).

    5—8. *and . . . die*   based on Holinshed's description of the "drunken
sleep" of the two "chamberlains" (see Appendix B, p. 171).

    5. *grooms*   servants.

    6. *charge*   i.e., of guarding the King.

    7. *that*   so that.

    8. S.D. *Enter* MACBETH   Macbeth's entry is usually placed (following
Steevens), after line 13, and his cry here marked "within." It is likely,
however, that he calls to his wife (see line 16), not to the sleepers
within, and that he is on-stage, exhausted and bloody, seen by the
audience but not at once by his wife, and slowly coming toward her.
Edwin Booth, the actor-producer, gave Macbeth's line here to one
of the grooms within.

    13. *husband*   the first and only time she so addresses him.

MACBETH

I have done the deed.—Did'st thou not hear a noise?

LADY MACBETH

15   I heard the owl scream and the crickets cry.
Did you not speak?

MACBETH

When?

LADY MACBETH

Now.

MACBETH

As I descended?

LADY MACBETH

Ay.

MACBETH

Hark!
Who lies i' th' second chamber?

LADY MACBETH

Donalbain.

MACBETH

20   This is a sorry sight.

LADY MACBETH

A foolish thought, to say a sorry sight.

MACBETH

There's one did laugh in's sleep, and one cried "Murder!"
That they did wake each other: I stood and heard them;

---

20. *this* i.e., the blood on his hands (see line 47).
23. *that* so that.

42

But they did say their prayers, and addressed them
Again to sleep.

LADY MACBETH

25   There are two lodged together.

MACBETH

One cried "God bless us," and "Amen" the other,
As they had seen me with these hangman's hands.
List'ning their fear, I could not say "Amen"
When they did say "God bless us."

LADY MACBETH

30   Consider it not so deeply.

MACBETH

But wherefore could I not pronounce "Amen"?
I had most need of blessing, and "Amen"
Stuck in my throat.

LADY MACBETH

These deeds must not be thought
After these ways; so, it will make us mad.

MACBETH

35   Methought I heard a voice cry "Sleep no more!
Macbeth does murder sleep!"—the innocent sleep,

---

24. *addressed them*   prepared themselves.

25. *two*   sometimes taken to be the grooms, sometimes Malcolm
and Donalbain.

27. *As*   as if. *hangman's hands*   The hangman's job included torture, and disemboweling and quartering his victims; his hands necessarily would be bloody.

28. *List'ning*   i.e., listening to, as at *Much Ado* III.i.12.

33. *thought*   Hanmer emended "thought" to "thought on," which
is the meaning here.

35–43. These lines recall conventional poetic ideas about sleep
stemming from Ovid (*Metamorphoses* XI.624) and given currency in
Elizabethan sonnets (see Philip Sidney's *Astrophel and Stella* XXXIX,

Sleep that knits up the ravelled sleave of care,
The death of each day's life, sore labour's bath,
Balm of hurt minds, great nature's second course,
Chief nourisher in life's feast.

LADY MACBETH

40   What do you mean?

MACBETH

Still it cried "Sleep no more!" to all the house:
"Glamis hath murdered sleep, and therefore Cawdor
Shall sleep no more, Macbeth shall sleep no more!"

LADY MACBETH

Who was it that thus cried? Why, worthy thane,
45   You do unbend your noble strength to think
So brain-sickly of things. Go, get some water,
And wash this filthy witness from your hand.—
Why did you bring these daggers from the place?
They must lie there; go, carry them, and smear
The sleepy grooms with blood.

MACBETH

50   I'll go no more:
I am afraid to think what I have done;
Look on't again I dare not.

"Come sleep, O sleep, the certain knot of peace, / The baiting-place
of wit, the balm of woe").

37. *ravelled sleave*   tangled thread; "sleave" = filament of silk.

39. *second course*   the main course at a meal, and the most nourish-
ing part of it.

45. *unbend*   Contrast I.vii.80–81, where he had "bent up" his
strength.

47. *witness*   evidence.

48. *daggers*   One stage tradition has Macbeth carry a dagger in
each hand in this scene (so David Garrick played it), but the fact that
Lady Macbeth does not notice the daggers until this line suggests that
he may at first conceal them.

LADY MACBETH

Infirm of purpose!

Give me the daggers. The sleeping and the dead
Are but as pictures; 'tis the eye of childhood

55   That fears a painted devil. If he do bleed,
I'll gild the faces of the grooms withal,
For it must seem their guilt.

Exit. Knock within.

MACBETH

Whence is that knocking?

How is't with me, when every noise appals me?
What hands are here? Ha! they pluck out mine eyes!

60   Will all great Neptune's ocean wash this blood
Clean from my hand? No. This my hand will rather
The multitudinous seas incarnadine,
Making the green one red.

Enter LADY MACBETH.

LADY MACBETH

My hands are of your colour, but I shame

65   To wear a heart so white. *(Knock)* I hear a knocking

56–7. *gild . . . guilt*   a grimly humorous pun; Shakespeare used it
elsewhere, as at 2 *Henry IV*, IV.v.129, but not with this force. As gold
was often called red, so blood could be thought of as golden (see
II.iii.116).

59. perhaps echoing Matthew 18:9, "And if thine eye offend thee,
pluck it out."

60–63. echoing Seneca, *Hippolytus*, 715–18; Macbeth's is the finest
and most famous rendering of an idea borrowed by other dramatists
of the period, as by John Marston, in *The Insatiate Countess* V.i, and
touched on earlier by Shakespeare himself, as in *Much Ado* IV.i.139–
43. F has at line 63 "Making the Greene one, Red," and the significance
of the comma and the question whether it should be there at all have
been much debated. Now it is usually taken as "making the green,
one red," but the line can be read either way.

65. *white*   cowardly.

At the south entry: retire we to our chamber;
A little water clears us of this deed.
How easy is it then! Your constancy
Hath left you unattended. *(Knock)* Hark, more knocking.
70   Get on your night-gown, lest occasion call us
And show us to be watchers; be not lost
So poorly in your thoughts.

MACBETH

                  To know my deed,
'Twere best not know myself.   *Knock.*
Wake Duncan with thy knocking; I would thou couldst!

                                        Exeunt.

Scene iii: Enter a Porter.

Knocking within.

PORTER

Here's a knocking indeed! If a man were porter of Hell gate,

65–9. *(Knock)* The parentheses are not in F, and are added to
mark off these stage directions from the text.

68–9. *Your . . . unattended* i.e., your firmness of purpose has
abandoned you, you have lost your nerve.

70. *night-gown* dressing gown.

72–3. *To . . . myself* i.e., it would be best not to be fully conscious
and rational if I am to face up to what I have done. (In other words, he
would rather be "lost" in thought than have to face the horrible fact
that he has murdered in cold blood).

Scene iii Coleridge was disgusted by this scene, which he regarded
as an interpolation "by some other hand," and his remarks on it have
provoked some notable defenses of its power, the most famous being
De Quincey's fine essay "On the Knocking at the Gate in *Macbeth*"
(see Introduction, p. xi). Producers of the play often make the Porter
drunk and noisily incoherent, perhaps, like Coleridge, regarding his
"low soliloquy" as mere comic relief; but his speeches are sharply
relevant to Macbeth and the murder of Duncan (see notes below).

he should have old turning the key. *(Knock)* Knock, knock,
knock. Who's there, i' th' name of Beelzebub? Here's a farmer
that hanged himself on th' expectation of plenty: come in,
5   farmer; have napkins enough about you, here you'll sweat
for't. *(Knock)* Knock, knock. Who's there, in th' other devil's
name? Faith, here's an equivocator that could swear in both
the scales against either scale, who committed treason enough
for God's sake, yet could not equivocate to Heaven: O come
10   in, equivocator. *(Knock)* Knock, knock, knock. Who's there?

2. *old*   plenty of, more than enough, as at *Much Ado* V.ii.83.

2, 6, 10, 13, 16. *(Knock)*   See II.ii.65, 69 and note.

3. *Beelzebub*   "the prince of the devils," Matthew 12:24.

3–4. *farmer . . . plenty*   an old joke referring to a farmer who
hoarded grain and realized, with the promise of a good harvest, that
corn would grow cheap and he would be ruined; but the farmer suggests Macbeth too, who, in the expectation of plenty (the crown), has
destroyed himself by murdering Duncan. Henry Garnet (see lines
7–9 and note) is said to have used the name "Farmer," and the line
may also be a quibbling allusion to him.

5. *farmer*   this seems the necessary emendation of "time" (F),
partly on the grounds of sense, partly on grounds of rhythm, as sup-
plying a word equivalent to "equivocator" (line 10), and "tailor" (line
12). Dover Wilson ingeniously suggests "time-server," which gives
good sense but does not belong in the repetitive rhythmic pattern of
the speech. *napkins*   handkerchiefs, as at *Othello* III.iii.291.

6–7. *th' other devil's name*   perhaps Satan, mentioned in Matthew
12:26 (see note to line 3), though properly Satan is the Devil.

7–9. *equivocator . . . Heaven*   equivocator: one who speaks with
duplicity; here implying Jesuit, owing to the ambiguities and prevarica-
tions to which the Roman Catholics were driven by the harsh penal
laws against them. There is almost certainly a specific allusion to the
trial in connection with the Gunpowder Plot of Henry Garnet, Superior
of the order of Jesuits in England, in March 1606, and to the use by
him of equivocation (or perjury, as his opponents called it) during the
interrogation (see Introduction, p. xvi). The "equivocator" also suggests Macbeth, who has juggled with words (as at I.iii.130ff.), and has
committed treason, but is to discover that he cannot "equivocate to
Heaven."

Faith, here's an English tailor come hither for stealing out of
a French hose: come in, tailor, here you may roast your goose.
(*Knock*) Knock, knock. Never at quiet. What are you?—but
this place is too cold for Hell. I'll devil-porter it no further; I

15 had thought to have let in some of all professions that go the
primrose way to th' everlasting bonfire. (*Knock*) Anon, anon;
I pray you, remember the porter.

[*He opens the gate.*]

Enter MACDUFF *and* LENNOX.

MACDUFF

Was it so late, friend, ere you went to bed,
That you do lie so late?

PORTER

20 Faith, sir, we were carousing till the second cock; and drink,
sir, is a great provoker of three things.

MACDUFF

What three things does drink especially provoke?

PORTER

Marry, sir, nose-painting, sleep, and urine. Lechery, sir, it
provokes, and unprovokes: it provokes the desire, but it takes

25 away the performance. Therefore, much drink may be said
to be an equivocator with lechery: it makes him, and it mars

---

12. *French hose* full round breeches, gartered below the knee.
The tailor could steal—with no one the wiser—by cheating the cus-
tomer on the amount of cloth used in making the breeches. Again
Macbeth may be indicated, who steals the crown and ends in hell.

12. *roast . . . goose* i.e., heat your smoothing iron (in hell fire).

16. *primrose . . . bonfire* See Matthew 7:13, "broad is the way, that
leadeth to destruction," and 25:41, "everlasting fire." Shakespeare
seems to have associated the primrose with the idea of an attractive,
flower-strewn way to hell (see *Hamlet* I.iii.50).

20. *second cock* second cockcrow. In *Romeo* IV.iv.3, this is equated
with three a.m.

23. *nose-painting* i.e., red noses.

him; it sets him on, and it takes him off; it persuades him, and
disheartens him; makes him stand to, and not stand to; in
conclusion, equivocates him in a sleep, and, giving him the
30   lie, leaves him.

MACDUFF

I believe drink gave thee the lie last night.

PORTER

That it did, sir, i' the very throat on me; but I requited him for
his lie, and, I think, being too strong for him, though he took
up my legs sometime, yet I made a shift to cast him.

MACDUFF

35   Is thy master stirring?

Enter MACBETH.

Our knocking has awaked him; here he comes.

LENNOX

Good morrow, noble sir.

MACBETH

         Good morrow, both.

MACDUFF

Is the King stirring, worthy thane?

MACBETH

           Not yet.

MACDUFF

He did command me to call timely on him;
I have almost slipped the hour.

29–30. *equivocates . . . him*   i.e., by making him fall asleep, dis-
ables and deceives him, at the same time giving him lascivious dreams.
    29–33. *giving . . . lie*   playing on two senses of "to give the lie":
to deceive, and to knock out or force to lie down.
    34. *cast*   throw (as in wrestling), and get rid of (by vomiting).
    40. *slipped*   let pass.

MACBETH

40   I'll bring you to him.

MACDUFF

I know this is a joyful trouble to you;
But yet 'tis one.

MACBETH

                The labour we delight in
Physics pain. This is the door.

MACDUFF

                    I'll make
So bold to call, for 'tis my limited service.

                                        Exit.

LENNOX

45 Goes the King hence today?

MACBETH

He does; he did appoint so.

LENNOX

The night has been unruly. Where we lay,
Our chimneys were blown down, and, as they say,
Lamentings heard i' th' air, strange screams of death,
50 And prophesying with accents terrible
Of dire combustion and confused events,
New-hatched to th' woeful time. The obscure bird
Clamoured the livelong night. Some say the earth
Was feverous and did shake.

MACBETH

                  'Twas a rough night.

---

43. *Physics* alleviates.
44. *limited service* assigned duty.
51. *combustion* tumult, disorder.
52. *obscure bird* i.e., the bird of darkness, the owl, a bird of ill omen (see II.ii.3 and note).

LENNOX

55 My young remembrance cannot parallel
A fellow to it.

Enter MACDUFF.

MACDUFF

O horror, horror, horror! Tongue nor heart
Cannot conceive nor name thee!

MACBETH *and* LENNOX
What's the matter?

MACDUFF

Confusion now hath made his masterpiece!
60 Most sacrilegious murder hath broke ope
The Lord's anointed temple, and stole thence
The life o' th' building.

MACBETH
What is't you say, the life?

LENNOX

Mean you his majesty?

MACDUFF

Approach the chamber, and destroy your sight
65 With a new Gorgon. Do not bid me speak:
See, and then speak yourselves; awake, awake!

Exeunt MACBETH *and* LENNOX.

Ring the alarum bell.—Murder and treason!
Banquo and Donalbain! Malcolm, awake!

60–61. *Most . . . temple* This brings together two common Biblical
ideas, one from the Old Testament, of the King as the "Lord's
anointed" (as at 2 Samuel 1:16), and the other of the body as the
"temple of God" (as at 1 Corinthians 3:16). The chapter in Samuel
concerns the slaying of King Saul.

65. *Gorgon* in Greek mythology, one of three sisters whose hair
was formed of snakes and whose look turned the beholder to stone.

Shake off this downy sleep, death's counterfeit,
70 And look on death itself! Up, up and see
The great doom's image! Malcolm, Banquo!
As from your graves rise up and walk like sprites
To countenance this horror! Ring the bell!

                                                    Bell rings.

            Enter LADY MACBETH.

                    LADY MACBETH

What's the business,
75 That such a hideous trumpet calls to parley
The sleepers of the house? Speak, speak!

                    MACDUFF

O gentle lady,
'Tis not for you to hear what I can speak;
The repetition in a woman's ear
Would murder as it fell.

                    Enter BANQUO.

80   O Banquo, Banquo,
Our royal master's murdered!

                    LADY MACBETH

                                    Woe, alas!
What, in our house?

                    BANQUO

                    Too cruel anywhere.
Dear Duff, I prithee contradict thyself,
And say it is not so.

---

71. *great doom's image* image of the Last Judgment (see *Lear*
V.iii.263–4).
72. *sprites* spirits, supernatural beings.
73. *countenance* be in keeping with. *Ring the bell!* possibly a
stage direction accidentally included in the text and then duplicated in
the margin. Lady Macbeth's first words, "What's the business," would
complete the line just as well; see below, pp. 178–9.

Enter MACBETH *and* LENNOX.

MACBETH

85 Had I but died an hour before this chance,
I had lived a blessèd time; for from this instant
There's nothing serious in mortality.
All is but toys; renown and grace is dead,
The wine of life is drawn, and the mere lees
90 Is left this vault to brag of.

Enter MALCOLM *and* DONALBAIN.

DONALBAIN

What is amiss?

MACBETH

You are, and do not know't.
The spring, the head, the fountain of your blood
Is stopped, the very source of it is stopped.

MACDUFF

Your royal father's murdered.

MALCOLM

O!—by whom?

---

84. S.D. *Enter . . .* LENNOX F adds "and Rosse," who has no speaking part in this scene, and who at this point is not of the inner councils (to judge from the questions he asks of Macduff in II.iv). Moreover, only Macbeth and Lennox went out to look at Duncan at line 66.

85. *chance* mischance, unhappy event.

87. *mortality* human existence.

88. *toys* trivialities. *renown . . . is dead* The two nouns form one idea, and the verb is singular.

90. *vault* bringing into play two senses of the word: "vault" as the sky (or "heaven's vault," as Lear calls it at V.iii.259), and hence by extension the world; and "vault" as a wine cellar.

94. *O! by whom?* Malcolm's first instinct is not to lament, but to discover who did it, and whether Malcolm himself, as heir, is also in danger.

LENNOX

95 Those of his chamber, as it seemed, had done't:
Their hands and faces were all badged with blood;
So were their daggers, which, unwiped, we found
Upon their pillows. They stared, and were distracted;
No man's life was to be trusted with them.

MACBETH

100 O yet I do repent me of my fury,
That I did kill them.

MACDUFF

Wherefore did you so?

MACBETH

Who can be wise, amazed, temp'rate and furious,
Loyal and neutral, in a moment? No man.
Th' expedition of my violent love

105 Outrun the pauser, reason. Here lay Duncan,
His silver skin laced with his golden blood,
And his gashed stabs looked like a breach in nature
For ruin's wasteful entrance; there the murderers,
Steeped in the colours of their trade, their daggers

110 Unmannerly breeched with gore. Who could refrain
That had a heart to love, and in that heart
Courage to make's love known?

---

106. *laced* streaked; from the interlacing colors used in embroidery (see *Romeo* III.v.7—8, "What envious streaks / Do lace the severing clouds in yonder east!"). *golden blood* See II.ii.56—7 and note.

107—8. *breach . . . entrance* The image is from a breach made by battering down fortification walls in war (see *Lear* IV.vii.15).

110. *unmannerly breeched* clothed (as with trousers, or breeches) indecently; i.e., the daggers are covered up to the hilts with gore.

LADY MACBETH

[*On the point of collapse*]   Help me hence, ho!

MACDUFF

Look to the lady.

[*Attendants go to her.*]

MALCOLM

[*To* DONALBAIN]   Why do we hold our tongues,
That most may claim this argument for ours?

DONALBAIN

115   [*To* MALCOLM] What should be spoken here, where our fate,
Hid in an auger-hole, may rush and seize us?
Let's away; our tears are not yet brewed.

MALCOLM

[*To* DONALBAIN] Nor our strong sorrow upon the foot of
motion.

BANQUO

Look to the lady!—

[LADY MACBETH *is escorted out.*]

---

112. Does Lady Macbeth really faint, or merely pretend to do so
in order to cover up what she sees as Macbeth's blunder in killing the
servants? The question has been much debated. The asides of Malcolm
and Donalbain are spoken while she is being revived.

114. *argument* theme for discussion (i.e., the murder of their
father).

116. *auger-hole* The term may have been picked up from Scot's
Discovery of Witchcraft I.iv.: "They [witches] can go in and out at
auger-holes." The thought may be of the difficulty of detecting so
tiny a hole (suggesting that treachery may lurk unnoticed in Macbeth's
castle), or of the smallness of the hole, or wound, necessary to stab a
man to death.

118. i.e., our sorrow has not yet begun to show itself.

120   And when we have our naked frailties hid,
That suffer in exposure, let us meet
And question this most bloody piece of work,
To know it further. Fears and scruples shake us:
In the great hand of God I stand, and thence
125   Against the undivulged pretence I fight
Of treasonous malice.

MACDUFF

And so do I.

ALL

So all.

MACBETH

Let's briefly put on manly readiness,
And meet i' th' hall together.

ALL

Well contented.

Exeunt [all but MALCOLM *and* DONALBAIN].

MALCOLM

What will you do? Let's not consort with them;
130   To show an unfelt sorrow is an office
Which the false man does easy. I'll to England.

DONALBAIN

To Ireland, I. Our separated fortune
Shall keep us both the safer; where we are

---

120. *naked frailties* All but Macduff and Lennox are wearing dressing gowns; "naked" means "unarmed, defenseless," rather than "unclothed."

125. *pretence* aim, or the purpose for which Duncan was murdered.

127. *manly readiness* suggesting not only that they should be dressed, but also armed.

129. *them* Malcolm and Donalbain suspect everyone.

131. *easy* easily.

There's daggers in men's smiles; the near in blood,
The nearer bloody.

MALCOLM

135   This murderous shaft that's shot
Hath not yet lighted, and our safest way
Is to avoid the aim. Therefore to horse,
And let us not be dainty of leave-taking,
But shift away: there's warrant in that theft
140   Which steals itself when there's no mercy left.

Exeunt.

Scene iv: Enter ROSS, *with an* Old Man.

OLD MAN

Threescore and ten I can remember well,
Within the volume of which time I have seen
Hours dreadful and things strange; but this sore night
Hath trifled former knowings.

134—5. *near . . . bloody* i.e., the nearer allied in blood, the more
likely to be murdered. He fears that the murderer will now strike at
them as Duncan's heirs.

138. *dainty of* particular about.

139—40. *theft . . . itself* Their "theft" consists in stealing away
from Macbeth's castle.

Scene iv The strange happenings that seem to symbolize the re-
bellion of Macbeth against the natural order—darkness, the falcon
killed by an owl, cannibal horses—all figure in Holinshed's account of
the murder of King Duff by Donwald (see Appendix B, p. 172). The
scene is not localized, and although it apparently takes place only a
few hours after II.iii, it also suggests a longer passage of time, for
Macbeth has gone to Scone and Duncan is in his grave (see lines 31—4).

3. *sore* terrible.

4. *trifled . . . knowings* made my earlier experience seem trifling.

ROSS

　　　　　　　　　　　Ha, good father,
5　Thou seest the heavens, as troubled with man's act,
Threatens his bloody stage. By th' clock 'tis day,
And yet dark night strangles the travelling lamp;
Is't night's predominance, or the day's shame,
That darkness does the face of earth entomb
When living light should kiss it?

OLD MAN

10　　　　　　　　　　　　'Tis unnatural,
Even like the deed that's done. On Tuesday last,
A falcon, towering in her pride of place,
Was by a mousing owl hawked at and killed.

ROSS

And Duncan's horses (a thing most strange and certain),
15　Beauteous and swift, the minions of their race,
Turned wild in nature, broke their stalls, flung out,
Contending 'gainst obedience, as they would
Make war with mankind.

OLD MAN

　　　　　　　　　'Tis said they ate each other.

---

6. *Threatens*　Another example of the common use of a singular verb with a plural subject.

7. *travelling lamp*　i.e., the sun moving across the sky.

8. *predominance*　ascendancy; in astrology the term refers to the superior influence of a planet. *shame*　i.e., at the murder of Duncan.

12. *towering . . . place*　having mounted to the point where the falcon is ready to swoop on its quarry. "Towering" and "place" are proper terms of falconry.

15. *minions*　the most pampered and finest animals; literally "darlings," or "favorites."

17. *as*　as if.

ROSS

They did so, to th' amazement of mine eyes
That looked upon't.

Enter MACDUFF.

20   Here comes the good Macduff.
How goes the world, sir, now?

MACDUFF

                         Why, see you not?

ROSS

Is't known who did this more than bloody deed?

MACDUFF

Those that Macbeth hath slain.

ROSS

                         Alas the day,
What good could they pretend?

MACDUFF

                         They were suborned.
25 Malcolm and Donalbain, the King's two sons,
Are stolen away and fled, which puts upon them
Suspicion of the deed.

ROSS

                    'Gainst nature still.
Thriftless ambition, that will raven up
Thine own life's means! Then 'tis most like
30 The sovereignty will fall upon Macbeth.

---

24. *pretend* hope for, intend. *suborned* i.e., bribed or paid to do
it.
27. *'Gainst . . . still* referring back to lines 10 and 16.
28. *raven up* devour greedily.

MACDUFF

He is already named, and gone to Scone
To be invested.

ROSS

Where is Duncan's body?

MACDUFF

Carried to Colmekill,
The sacred storehouse of his predecessors,
And guardian of their bones.

ROSS

35   Will you to Scone?

MACDUFF

No, cousin, I'll to Fife.

ROSS

Well, I will thither.

MACDUFF

Well, may you see things well done there—adieu—
Lest our old robes sit easier than our new!

ROSS

Farewell, father.

---

31. *Scone* The Abbey of Scone (pronounced "Skoon"), where the
kings of Scotland were crowned, lay about two miles north of Perth.
The famous Stone of Destiny, on which the coronation rites were performed, was taken from Scone by Edward I of England in 1296 and
transferred to Westminster Abbey. It is now enclosed in the coronation chair used by British monarchs.

33. *Colmekill* An old name for Iona, a tiny island in the Hebrides
where the ancient kings of Scotland were buried.

36. *Fife* In eastern Scotland (see map, p. xxviii). Macduff chooses
to go home to his own castle. *thither* i.e., to Scone.

38. *lest . . . new!* i.e., in case things change for the worse and they
are not able to exchange such friendly greetings again.

OLD MAN

40 God's benison go with you, and with those
    That would make good of bad, and friends of foes.

                                Exeunt.

Act III, scene i: Enter BANQUO.

BANQUO

Thou hast it now, King, Cawdor, Glamis, all,
As the Weird Women promised, and I fear
Thou play'dst most foully for't; yet it was said
It should not stand in thy posterity,
5 But that myself should be the root and father
Of many kings. If there come truth from them—
As upon thee, Macbeth, their speeches shine—
Why, by the verities on thee made good,
May they not be my oracles as well,
10 And set me up in hope? But hush, no more.

---

40. *benison* blessing.

scene i Act II, scene iv, helped to bridge the interval of time between the murder, Macbeth's coronation (II.iv.31), and his establish-
ment on the throne. Now Malcolm is in England and Donalbain in
Ireland (lines 29–30), and Macbeth holds court, presumably at Forres
(see I.iv and note).

1–10. Holinshed reports that Banquo was Macbeth's accomplice
in the murder of Duncan (see Appendix B, p. 164); but it would not
have been politic—or dramatically as effective—for Shakespeare to
have directly involved Banquo in the murder, since Banquo was
James I's ancestor. However, A.C. Bradley, in *Shakespearean Tragedy*,
pp. 384–5, suggests that Banquo here becomes an accessory after the
fact because although he suspects foul play, he keeps silent about
the Witches and, swayed by his own ambitions, fails to expose
Macbeth.

4. *It . . . stand* i.e., the succession should not endure.

7. *their speeches shine* i.e., what they said has conspicuously come
to pass.

Sennet sounded. Enter MACBETH, *as King,* LADY [MACBETH],
    LENNOX, ROSS, *lords and attendants.*

MACBETH

Here's our chief guest.

LADY MACBETH

            If he had been forgotten,
It had been as a gap in our great feast,
And all-thing unbecoming.

MACBETH

Tonight we hold a solemn supper, sir,
And I'll request your presence.

BANQUO

15   Let your highness
Command upon me, to the which my duties
Are with a most indissoluble tie
Forever knit.

MACBETH

Ride you this afternoon?

BANQUO

            Ay, my good lord.

---

10. S.D. *Sennet*   a fanfare played on trumpets (a variant of "signet" in the sense of "sign," or "signal").

13. *all-thing*   wholly.

14. *solemn*   formal, indicating that the supper would be a ceremonious banquet.

16. *Command upon*   telescoping the phrase "lay your command upon me."

17–18. *Are . . . knit*   Is this mere good manners, or deliberate hypocrisy? See lines 1–10 above and note.

MACBETH

20 We should have else desired your good advice—
Which still hath been both grave and prosperous—
In this day's council; but we'll take tomorrow.
Is't far you ride?

BANQUO

As far, my lord, as will fill up the time
25 'Twixt this and supper. Go not my horse the better,
I must become a borrower of the night
For a dark hour or twain.

MACBETH

           Fail not our feast.

BANQUO

My lord, I will not.

MACBETH

We hear our bloody cousins are bestowed
30 In England and in Ireland, not confessing
Their cruel parricide, filling their hearers
With strange invention.—But of that tomorrow,
When therewithal we shall have cause of state
Craving us jointly. Hie you to horse: adieu,
35 Till you return at night.—Goes Fleance with you?

BANQUO

Ay, my good lord. Our time does call upon's.

---

21. *Which . . . prosperous*   which has ever been both serious and profitable.

25. *Go . . . better*   i.e., if my horse does not go fast enough; a common construction.

33. *cause of state*   affairs of state, government business.

36. *upon's*   i.e., upon us.

MACBETH

I wish your horses swift and sure of foot;
And so I do commend you to their backs.
Farewell.

Exit BANQUO.

40 Let every man be master of his time
Till seven at night;
To make society the sweeter welcome,
We will keep ourself till supper-time alone.
While then, God be with you.

Exeunt [*all but* MACBETH *and a* Servant].
Sirrah, a word with you.
Attend those men our pleasure?

SERVANT

They are, my lord,

45 Without the palace gate.

MACBETH

Bring them before us.

Exit Servant.

To be thus is nothing,
But to be safely thus. Our fears in Banquo
Stick deep, and in his royalty of nature

41–2. *night; . . . welcome,* Theobald's punctuation; F has "Night,
. . . welcome:" which breaks the rhythm and makes poor sense, since
it destroys the connection between solitude and the pleasures of
society.

44. *While* until.

47–8. *To . . . safely thus* i.e., to be king in name is nothing; to be
safe as king is what matters.

49. *Stick deep* are deeply grounded. *royalty* Perhaps Shakespeare meant this as a compliment to James I, Banquo's descendant;
see above lines 1–10, 17–18 and notes, and also Introduction, pp.
xv–xvi.

50 Reigns that which would be feared. 'Tis much he dares,
    And to that dauntless temper of his mind
    He hath a wisdom that doth guide his valour
    To act in safety. There is none but he
    Whose being I do fear; and under him
55 My genius is rebuked, as it is said
    Mark Antony's was by Caesar. He chid the Sisters
    When first they put the name of King upon me,
    And bade them speak to him. Then, prophet-like,
    They hailed him father to a line of kings.
60 Upon my head they placed a fruitless crown,
    And put a barren scepter in my gripe,
    Thence to be wrenched with an unlineal hand,
    No son of mine succeeding. If't be so,
    For Banquo's issue have I filed my mind;
65 For them the gracious Duncan have I murdered;
    Put rancours in the vessel of my peace
    Only for them; and mine eternal jewel
    Given to the common enemy of man,
    To make them kings, the seeds of Banquo kings!
70 Rather than so, come, Fate, into the list,

54–6. *under . . . Caesar* referring to a passage in Plutarch's life of Antony, which is paraphrased in *Antony and Cleopatra* II.iii.17–23. The "genius" is the attendant spirit who, as the Romans thought, governed a person's fortune.

56. *chid the Sisters* See I.iii.52ff.

64. *filed* defiled.

66. filled the cup of my peace with bitter enmity. The image is adapted from a common Biblical metaphor: see, for instance, Psalms 75:8, "in the hand of the Lord there is a cup and the wine is red . . . and he poureth out of the same: as for the dregs thereof, all the ungodly of the earth . . . shall drink them" (*Book of Common Prayer*).

67. *eternal jewel* i.e., immortal soul. The passage may echo Mark 8:36, "What shall it profit a man, if he shall gain the whole world, and lose his own soul?"

70–71. *come . . . utterance* i.e., come, Fate, into the place of battle

And champion me to th' utterance!—Who's there?

Enter Servant *and two* Murderers.

[*To the* Servant] Now go to the door, and stay there till we call.

                                   Exit Servant.

Was it not yesterday we spoke together?

MURDERERS

It was, so please your highness.

MACBETH

                     Well then now,

75   Have you considered of my speeches? Know
That it was he, in the times past, which held you
So under fortune, which you thought had been
Our innocent self. This I made good to you
In our last conference, passed in probation with you
80   How you were borne in hand, how crossed, the instruments,
Who wrought with them, and all things else that might
To half a soul and to a notion crazed
Say, "Thus did Banquo."

FIRST MURDERER

You made it known to us.

---

and fight beside me to the bitter end (or to the death). Macbeth's words are usually taken as a challenge to Fate (based on the now obsolete definition of "champion" as "to challenge to a combat"), but the lines can also be interpreted as an invitation to Fate to stand on Macbeth's side, or to "champion" him in the more usual sense of the word.

71. S.D. *Murderers* They are not yet murderers but, by their own claim, ruined men (see lines 108ff.).

75. *considered of* given heed to; once common usage, this expression still survives in British speech.

77. *under fortune* below the success (good fortune) you deserved.

79. *passed in probation* went over the proofs.

80. *borne in hand* cheated with false hopes. *crossed* thwarted. *the instruments* the means.

82. *notion* mind.

MACBETH

85 I did so; and went further, which is now
    Our point of second meeting. Do you find
    Your patience so predominant in your nature
    That you can let this go? Are you so gospelled
    To pray for this good man and for his issue,
90 Whose heavy hand hath bowed you to the grave
    And beggared yours forever?

FIRST MURDERER

                We are men, my liege.

MACBETH

    Ay, in the catalogue ye go for men,
    As hounds and greyhounds, mongrels, spaniels, curs,
    Shoughs, water-rugs, and demi-wolves, are clept
95 All by the name of dogs. The valued file
    Distinguishes the swift, the slow, the subtle,
    The housekeeper, the hunter, every one
    According to the gift which bounteous nature
    Hath in him closed; whereby he does receive
100 Particular addition, from the bill
    That writes them all alike; and so of men.
    Now, if you have a station in the file,
    Not i' th' worst rank of manhood, say't;
    And I will put that business in your bosoms

88–9. *gospelled . . . issue* The gospel is from Matthew 5:44, "Love your enemies, bless them that curse you, do good to them that hate you, and pray for them which despitefully use you, and persecute you."

94. *Shoughs, water-rugs, and demi-wolves* rough mongrel lap-dogs, shaggy water-dogs (dogs used for fowling), and animals that are half dog, half wolf. *clept* called.

95. *valued file* list showing values, or price list.

99. *closed* enclosed.

100. *addition* distinction, as at I.iii.106. *bill* catalogue.

104. *bosoms* i.e., as the repository of secret counsels.

105   Whose execution takes your enemy off,
Grapples you to the heart and love of us,
Who wear our health but sickly in his life,
Which in his death were perfect.

SECOND MURDERER

                I am one, my liege,
Whom the vile blows and buffets of the world
110   Hath so incensed that I am reckless what
I do to spite the world.

FIRST MURDERER

           And I another,
So weary with disasters, tugged with fortune,
That I would set my life on any chance,
To mend it or to be rid on't.

MACBETH

           Both of you
Know Banquo was your enemy.

MURDERERS

115   True, my lord.

MACBETH

So is he mine; and in such bloody distance
That every minute of his being thrusts
Against my near'st of life; and though I could
With barefaced power sweep him from my sight

---

107. *in his life*   i.e., while he lives.
109–10. *blows . . . Hath*   See I.iii.148 and note.
112. *tugged with*   mauled by.
116. *distance*   enmity (from the Latin *distantia*—"standing apart," or "separation").
118. *near'st of life*   i.e., most vital parts, all that most closely concerns him.

120 And bid my will avouch it, yet I must not,
  For certain friends that are both his and mine,
  Whose loves I may not drop, but wail his fall
  Who I myself struck down; and thence it is
  That I to your assistance do make love,
125 Masking the business from the common eye
  For sundry weighty reasons.

      SECOND MURDERER
          We shall, my lord,
  Perform what you command us.

      FIRST MURDERER
          Though our lives—

      MACBETH
  Your spirits shine through you. Within this hour at most
  I will advise you where to plant yourselves,
130 Acquaint you with the perfect spy o' th' time,
  The moment on't, for't must be done tonight,
  And something from the palace; always thought
  That I require a clearness; and with him,

---

120. *bid . . . it* i.e., let my will and pleasure be sufficient sanction for it.

122. *but wail* i.e., but (I must) bewail.

123. *Who* for "whom," as is still common in colloquial speech (see Abbott, 274).

130. *perfect . . . time* exact notice of the time to act. But Dr. Johnson supposed that the word "spy," rather than meaning "espyal" (i.e., "notice"), referred to the Third Murderer, who appears in III.iii.

131. *on't* i.e., of it.

132. *something* i.e., some distance. *always thought* i.e., it must be kept in mind.

133. *clearness* "That in time to come he might clear himself, if anything were laid to his charge" is Holinshed's phrase (see Appendix B, p. 165).

To leave no rubs nor botches in the work,
135 Fleance his son, that keeps him company,
Whose absence is no less material to me
Than is his father's, must embrace the fate
Of that dark hour. Resolve yourselves apart;
I'll come to you anon.

MURDERERS

We are resolved, my lord.

MACBETH

140 I'll call upon you straight. Abide within.

[*Exeunt* Murderers.]

It is concluded. Banquo, thy soul's flight,
If it find Heaven, must find it out tonight.

Exit.

Scene ii: Enter LADY MACBETH *and a* Servant.

LADY MACBETH

Is Banquo gone from court?

SERVANT

Ay, madam, but returns again tonight.

LADY MACBETH

Say to the King, I would attend his leisure
For a few words.

SERVANT

Madam, I will.   *Exit.*

---

134. *leave . . . work*   leave no roughness or blemishes in the work,
make a clean job of it.

138. *Resolve yourselves*   make up your minds.

Scene ii   There is no break in time. Lady Macbeth enters as in another part of the palace.

LADY MACBETH

                         Nought's had, all's spent,

5   Where our desire is got without content:
'Tis safer to be that which we destroy,
Than by destruction dwell in doubtful joy.

Enter MACBETH.

How now, my lord? Why do you keep alone,
Of sorriest fancies your companions making,
10   Using those thoughts which should indeed have died
With them they think on? Things without all remedy
Should be without regard: what's done is done.

MACBETH

We have scorched the snake, not killed it:
She'll close and be herself, whilst our poor malice
15   Remains in danger of her former tooth.
But let the frame of things disjoint, both the worlds suffer,
Ere we will eat our meal in fear, and sleep
In the affliction of these terrible dreams
That shake us nightly. Better be with the dead,

6–7. She is as disillusioned as Macbeth (see III.i.47–8).

9. *sorriest* most dismal. She knows he is brooding on the murder of Duncan.

10. *Using* keeping company with.

12. *what's . . . done* Compare her remark at V.i.55, "What's done cannot be undone."

13. *scorched* slashed, as with a knife (a variant of the modern "score," meaning "cut"); Theobald's eighteenth-century emendation to "scotched," which has gained wide currency as a familiar quotation, is quite unwarranted.

15. *tooth* i.e., sting, or power of hurting; and see III.iv. 28–30.

16. i.e., but let the universe fall apart, both the (terrestrial and celestial) worlds suffer. The line itself is disjointed, and the disturbance of the verse pattern by this long line, or fragments of two lines, emphasizes Macbeth's passion.

20   Whom we, to gain our peace, have sent to peace,
     Than on the torture of the mind to lie
     In restless ecstasy. Duncan is in his grave;
     After life's fitful fever he sleeps well.
     Treason has done his worst. Nor steel, nor poison,
25   Malice domestic, foreign levy, nothing
     Can touch him further.

LADY MACBETH
           Come on.
     Gentle my lord, sleek o'er your rugged looks;
     Be bright and jovial among your guests tonight.

MACBETH
     So shall I, love, and so I pray, be you.
30   Let your remembrance apply to Banquo;
     Present him eminence, both with eye and tongue—
     Unsafe the while that we
     Must lave our honours in these flattering streams,
     And make our faces vizards to our hearts,
     Disguising what they are.

LADY MACBETH
35   You must leave this.

---

20. *our peace* i.e., the peace of mind, or happiness, he expected to find by satisfying his ambition to be king.

21. *lie* as if being tortured on the rack.

22. *ecstasy* i.e., frenzy of anxiety.

25. *levy* i.e., raising of troops to make war on Duncan.

30. *remembrance* pronounced "rememberance."

31. *Present him eminence* give him special distinction.

32–3. *Unsafe . . . streams* i.e., we are unsafe as long as we can keep our honor bright only by bathing it in streams of flattery to Banquo.

34. *vizards* masks.

MACBETH

O, full of scorpions is my mind, dear wife!
Thou know'st that Banquo and his Fleance lives.

LADY MACBETH

But in them nature's copy's not eterne.

MACBETH

There's comfort yet, they are assailable;
40   Then be thou jocund. Ere the bat hath flown
His cloistered flight, ere to black Hecate's summons
The shard-born beetle with his drowsy hums
Hath rung night's yawning peal, there shall be done
A deed of dreadful note.

LADY MACBETH

What's to be done?

---

37. *lives*   See I.iii.148 and note.

38. *copy's*   probably used in the sense of "counterpart"; man is made in the image of God (Genesis 1:26), but since his body is only nature's copy, or counterpart, of that image, he is subject to death (see *Othello* V.ii.11). The word has also often been taken as meaning "copyhold," or the tenure under which men hold their lives from nature.

40–43. *bat . . . peal*   The bat is proverbially blind and a creature of darkness; the beetle, too, is proverbially blind and associated with blackness (see *M.N. Dream* II.ii.22); both are here linked with Hecate, goddess of witchcraft (see II.i.51–2). Macbeth is gathering strength for the invocation beginning at line 46, and shedding on the way the sweeter associations of the night with peace ("cloistered") and sleep ("drowsy hums").

42. *shard-born*   bred in shards, or dung. There seems to be no real basis for the common—and attractive—interpretation "borne on horny wings."

44. *note*   notoriety.

MACBETH

45   Be innocent of the knowledge, dearest chuck,
      Till thou applaud the deed. Come, seeling night,
      Scarf up the tender eye of pitiful day,
      And with thy bloody and invisible hand
      Cancel and tear to pieces that great bond
50   Which keeps me pale. Light thickens, and the crow
      Makes wing to th' rooky wood.
      Good things of day begin to droop and drowse,
      Whiles night's black agents to their preys do rouse.
      Thou marvell'st at my words: but hold thee still;
55   Things bad begun make strong themselves by ill.
      So prithee go with me.

                                          Exeunt.

---

45. *chuck*   an intimate term of endearment (probably a variant of "chick").

46. *seeling*   blinding; in falconry the term means to stitch closed the eyelids of a hawk (in order to tame it). See the remarks on "bat" and "beetle" in the note to lines 40–43 above.

49. *Cancel . . . bond*   i.e., cancel the obligation of love and loyalty to his subjects and other men generally (see Leviticus 29:18 and Matthew 5:43–4). The phrase, as a legal metaphor, may have been suggested by the pun in "seeling" / "sealing."

50–51. *crow . . . wood*   Crows and rooks link with the bat and beetle imagery of lines 40 and 42 above to give concrete force to the phrase "night's black agents" (line 53). There has been much discussion of the exact meaning of the line: see, for example, William Empson, *Seven Types of Ambiguity* (London, 1930), pp. 25, 103.

55. *Things . . . ill*   A "sentence," or moral tag, similar to Seneca's *Agamemnon*, line 115, which is spoken by a tyrant: *Per scelera semper sceleribus tutum est iter* (The safe path to evil deeds is always through evil deeds).

Scene iii: Enter three Murderers.

FIRST MURDERER

But who did bid thee join with us?

THIRD MURDERER

Macbeth.

SECOND MURDERER

He needs not our mistrust, since he delivers
Our offices and what we have to do
To the direction just.

FIRST MURDERER

Then stand with us.
5   The west yet glimmers with some streaks of day.
Now spurs the lated traveller apace
To gain the timely inn, and near approaches
The subject of our watch.

THIRD MURDERER

Hark! I hear horses.

BANQUO [*within*]

Give us a light there, ho!

Scene iii   The setting, outside the palace, is created in the verse
(lines 5–8).
S.D. *Enter* . . . Murderers   When Laurence Olivier played Macbeth,
he had the two Murderers close in on him, at III.i.74, on the phrase
"Well then now"; huddled together in their black cloaks, the three
men reminded the audience of the three Witches. Here Shakespeare
again emphasizes a dark trio by introducing the Third Murderer.
Some critics have identified him with Macbeth, Ross, or various others,
but such speculation seems pointless.
2. *He . . . mistrust*   i.e., we need not mistrust the Third Murderer.
4. *To . . . just*   i.e., exactly according to Macbeth's instructions.

SECOND MURDERER

Then 'tis he; the rest

10 That are within the note of expectation
Already are i' th' court.

FIRST MURDERER

His horses go about.

THIRD MURDERER

Almost a mile; but he does usually,
So all men do, from hence to th' palace gate
Make it their walk.

Enter BANQUO *and* FLEANCE *with a torch.*

SECOND MURDERER

A light, a light!

THIRD MURDERER

'Tis he.

FIRST MURDERER

15 Stand to't.

BANQUO

It will be rain tonight.

FIRST MURDERER

Let it come down.

[*Strikes out the light and stabs* BANQUO.]

BANQUO

O treachery! Fly, good Fleance, fly, fly, fly!
Thou may'st revenge. O slave!

[*Dies.* FLEANCE *escapes.*]

---

10. *note of expectation*   list of expected guests.

THIRD MURDERER

Who did strike out the light?

FIRST MURDERER

Was't not the way?

THIRD MURDERER

There's but one down; the son is fled.

SECOND MURDERER

20   We have lost
Best half of our affair.

FIRST MURDERER

Well, let's away, and say how much is done.

Exeunt.

Scene iv: Banquet prepared. Enter MACBETH, LADY [MACBETH],
ROSS, LENNOX, *lords and attendants.*

MACBETH

You know your own degrees; sit down. At first
And last, the hearty welcome.

LORDS

Thanks to your majesty.

Scene iv For this scene, inside the palace, a table and chairs are
brought on-stage, including "chairs of state," or raised chairs with
canopies, for Lady Macbeth and Macbeth.

1. *You . . . degrees* emphasizing the formal nature of the feast;
the guests sit in order of rank and precedence.

1–2. *At . . . last* i.e., once and for all.

MACBETH

Ourself will mingle with society
And play the humble host.

5   Our hostess keeps her state, but in best time
We will require her welcome.

LADY MACBETH

Pronounce it for me, sir, to all our friends,
For my heart speaks they are welcome.

Enter First Murderer [*to one side*].

MACBETH

See, they encounter thee with their hearts' thanks.

10   Both sides are even; here I'll sit i' th' midst.
Be large in mirth; anon, we'll drink a measure
The table round.

[*He notices the* Murderer *and goes to him.*]
There's blood upon thy face.

MURDERER

'Tis Banquo's then.

MACBETH

'Tis better thee without than he within.
Is he dispatched?

MURDERER

15   My lord, his throat is cut;
That I did for him.

3—5. *Ourself . . . state* Macbeth comes down from his chair of
state, but Lady Macbeth remains aloof from her guests.

6. *require* request.

10. *Both . . . midst* the numbers on each side of the table are
equal. One place remains for Macbeth, presumably at the end, where
he is "i' th' midst," i.e., between the two sides.

14. *better . . . within* i.e., better on you than in his body.

MACBETH

Thou art the best o' th' cutthroats;
Yet he's good that did the like for Fleance:
If thou didst it, thou art the nonpareil.

MURDERER

Most royal sir—Fleance is 'scaped.

MACBETH

20 [*Aside*] Then comes my fit again. I had else been perfect,
Whole as the marble, founded as the rock,
As broad and general as the casing air.
But now I am cabined, cribbed, confined, bound in
To saucy doubts and fears. [*To* Murderer] But Banquo's safe?

MURDERER

25 Ay, my good lord; safe in a ditch he bides,
With twenty trenchèd gashes on his head,
The least a death to nature.

MACBETH

Thanks for that.—
There the grown serpent lies; the worm that's fled
Hath nature that in time will venom breed,
30 No teeth for th' present.—Get thee gone; tomorrow
We'll hear ourselves again.

Exit Murderer.

---

18. *the nonpareil* without equal.
21. *founded . . . rock* See Matthew 7:24–5, where faith is said to be "founded upon a rock" (Authorized Version; "grounded on a rock" in the Bishop's and Geneva Bibles).
22. *broad and general* free and unconfined. *casing* surrounding.
23. *cribbed* shut up as in a hovel (see 2 *Henry IV*, III.i.9).
24. *safe* i.e., beyond the power of doing harm.
26. *trenchèd* deep-cut.
28. *worm* snake, or serpent.
30. *teeth* See III.ii.15 and note.
31. *hear ourselves* i.e., talk with each other.

LADY MACBETH

My royal lord,
You do not give the cheer. The feast is sold
That is not often vouched, while 'tis a-making,
'Tis given with welcome. To feed were best at home;
35 From thence, the sauce to meat is ceremony;
Meeting were bare without it.

Enter the Ghost of Banquo, *and sits in* MACBETH's *place.*

MACBETH

[*To her*]   Sweet remembrancer!
[*To the company*] Now good digestion wait on appetite,
And health on both!

LENNOX

May't please your highness sit?

32–4. *You . . . home* i.e., you do not make your guests welcome;
the feast is sold (not given) at which the host does not frequently as-
sure his guests, during the meal, that it is given with welcome. In
such a case they might just as well eat at home.

35. *From thence* i.e., away from home.

36. S.D. *the* Ghost Simon Forman, who saw the play at the Globe
Theatre in 1610 (see Appendix D, p. 175), reports that the Ghost of
Banquo "came and sat down in his [Macbeth's] chair," and the usual
stage practice is still to bring on an actor impersonating the Ghost.
Some great actor-directors, however—among them John Kemble
(1786) and Edwin Booth (1828)—have not represented the Ghost
physically on the stage, treating him rather as a specter of Macbeth's
overwrought mind. The entrance is often placed by editors after line
40, but its placing in F allows the actor time to walk to the table as the
next few lines are spoken. Although F marks the entrance of the
Ghost here and at line 87, it gives no exits for him.

36. *remembrancer* one who reminds. He looks at his wife, but the
audience sees another "remembrancer," the Ghost of Banquo.

MACBETH

Here had we now our country's honour roofed,
40 Were the graced person of our Banquo present;
Who may I rather challenge for unkindness
Than pity for mischance!

ROSS

His absence, sir,
Lays blame upon his promise. Please't your highness
To grace us with your royal company?

MACBETH

The table's full.

LENNOX

45 Here is a place reserved, sir.

MACBETH

Where?

LENNOX

Here, my good lord. What is't that moves your highness?

MACBETH

Which of you have done this?

LORDS

What, my good lord?

MACBETH

[*To the* Ghost] Thou canst not say I did it; never shake
50 Thy gory locks at me.

---

39. *our . . . roofed* our country's men of distinction under our roof.

40. *graced* honored, gracious.

41. *who* i.e., whom, as at III.i.123.

45. *The . . . full* At first he does not notice the presence of Banquo's shade but merely that no seat is empty.

49. *did it* i.e., killed Banquo.

ROSS

Gentlemen, rise; his highness is not well.

LADY MACBETH

Sit, worthy friends. My lord is often thus,
And hath been from his youth. Pray you, keep seat;
The fit is momentary, upon a thought
55   He will again be well. If much you note him
You shall offend him and extend his passion;
Feed, and regard him not. [*To* MACBETH] Are you a man?

MACBETH

Ay, and a bold one, that dare look on that
Which might appal the Devil.

LADY MACBETH

                              O proper stuff!
60   This is the very painting of your fear;
This is the air-drawn dagger which you said
Led you to Duncan. O these flaws and starts—
Impostors to true fear—would well become
A woman's story at a winter's fire,
65   Authorized by her grandam. Shame itself!
Why do you make such faces? When all's done
You look but on a stool.

---

54. *upon a thought*   in no time.

56. *offend . . . passion*   do harm to him and prolong his outburst.

59. *proper stuff!*   excellent nonsense! She is, of course, speaking
scornfully.

61. *air-drawn*   a pun: painted in the air, and drawn through the
air (see II.i.33).

62. *flaws*   sudden fits of passion (literally, gusts of wind).

63. *to*   i.e., compared to.

65. *authorized*   vouched for.

MACBETH

Prithee, see there!

Behold! look! lo! how say you?

Why, what care I? [To the Ghost] If thou canst nod, speak too.

70   If charnel houses and our graves must send

Those that we bury back, our monuments

Shall be the maws of kites.

[Exit Ghost.]

LADY MACBETH

What! quite unmanned in folly?

MACBETH

If I stand here, I saw him.

LADY MACBETH

Fie, for shame!

MACBETH

Blood hath been shed ere now, i' th' olden time,

75   Ere humane statute purged the gentle weal;

Ay, and since too, murders have been performed

Too terrible for the ear. The time has been

That, when the brains were out, the man would die,

And there an end; but now they rise again,

71–2. *our . . . kites*   our tombs shall be the bellies of birds of prey;
i.e., it would be safer for the dead to be devoured so that they cannot
return to haunt us. Dover Wilson quotes from Scot, *Discovery of
Witchcraft* V.vi: "After the death of Nebuchadnezzar, his son . . . gave
his body to the ravens to be devoured, lest afterwards his father should
arise from death."

74–82. Macbeth talks to himself, brooding on what he has seen.

75. *humane*   meaning both "human" and "humane"; the words
were not distinguished until the 18th century. *purged . . . weal*   freed
the state from bloodshed, and made it gentle (or peaceful). For the
construction, see I.vi.3 and note.

80 With twenty mortal murders on their crowns,
And push us from our stools. This is more strange
Than such a murder is.

LADY MACBETH
My worthy lord,
Your noble friends do lack you.

MACBETH
I do forget.
[*To the company*] Do not muse at me, my most worthy friends;
85 I have a strange infirmity, which is nothing
To those that know me. Come, love and health to all,
Then I'll sit down. Give me some wine, fill full.

Enter Ghost.

I drink to th' general joy o' th' whole table,
And to our dear friend Banquo, whom we miss.
90 Would he were here! To all, and him, we thirst,
And all to all.

LORDS
Our duties, and the pledge.

MACBETH
[*To the* Ghost] Avaunt, and quit my sight! Let the earth hide
thee!
Thy bones are marrowless, thy blood is cold;
Thou hast no speculation in those eyes
Which thou dost glare with.

---

80. *twenty . . . crowns*   referring to the "trenchèd gashes" of lines
26–7 above.
90. *thirst*   long for.
91. *all to all*   i.e., let all drink to one another.
94. *speculation*   light of intelligence.

84

LADY MACBETH

95   Think of this, good peers,
But as a thing of custom; 'tis no other,
Only it spoils the pleasure of the time.

MACBETH

What man dare, I dare.
Approach thou like the rugged Russian bear,
100   The armed rhinoceros, or th' Hyrcan tiger;
Take any shape but that, and my firm nerves
Shall never tremble. Or be alive again,
And dare me to the desert with thy sword;
If trembling I inhabit then, protest me
105   The baby of a girl. Hence, horrible shadow!
Unreal mock'ry, hence!

                            [*Exit* Ghost.]

            Why, so; being gone,
I am a man again. [*To the company*] Pray you, sit still.

LADY MACBETH

You have displaced the mirth, broke the good meeting
With most admired disorder.

---

98. This half-line seems to continue from Macbeth's last speech, as though he does not hear Lady Macbeth at all here.

100. *Hyrcan* Hyrcania, an area south of the Caspian Sea, was named by Pliny in his *Natural History* (translated into English in 1601) as a place where tigers were bred.

103. *to the desert* i.e., where they would be alone, man to man.

104. *If . . . then* not explained; perhaps "if I *remain here* trembling then," or "if I *harbor* any fears then." For this latter usage of "inhabit," Dover Wilson compares *As You Like It* III.iii.7–8, "O knowledge, ill-inhabited, worse than Jove in a thatched house!" *protest* proclaim.

105. *baby of a girl* i.e., babyish girl (as "he's a fool of a man" = "he's a foolish man").

109. *admired* wondered at (the original meaning, from the Latin *admirari*).

MACBETH

               Can such things be
110 And overcome us like a summer's cloud,
Without our special wonder? You make me strange
Even to the disposition that I owe,
When now I think you can behold such sights
And keep the natural ruby of your cheeks
When mine is blanched with fear.

ROSS

115   What sights, my lord?

LADY MACBETH

I pray you, speak not. He grows worse and worse;
Question enrages him. At once, good night.
Stand not upon the order of your going,
But go at once.

LENNOX

       Good night, and better health
Attend his majesty!

LADY MACBETH

120   A kind good night to all!

                 Exeunt lords [and attendants].

MACBETH

It will have blood, they say: blood will have blood.

---

110. *overcome*   meaning both "overwhelm" and "pass over."

111–12. *You . . . owe*   i.e., you make me feel that I do not know my own frame of mind ("owe" = "own"). He doubts his own courage, seeing everyone else unmoved.

118–19. *Stand . . . once*   disorder contrasting with their orderly entrance (see line 1 and note above).

121. The idea is proverbial (Tilley, B—458), and stems from Genesis 9:6 "Whoso sheddeth man's blood, by man shall his blood be shed."

Stones have been known to move and trees to speak;
Auguries and understood relations have
By maggot-pies and choughs and rooks brought forth
125 The secret'st man of blood. What is the night?

LADY MACBETH

Almost at odds with morning, which is which.

MACBETH

How say'st thou, that Macduff denies his person
At our great bidding?

LADY MACBETH
Did you send to him, sir?

MACBETH

I hear it by the way; but I will send.
130 There's not a one of them but in his house
I keep a servant fee'd. I will tomorrow—
And betimes I will—to the Weird Sisters.
More shall they speak; for now I am bent to know,

---

122. i.e., to reveal blood guilt. The stones are usually explained as gravestones on the tombs of murdered men; the idea of a speaking tree goes back to Virgil, *Aeneid* III. 22–68, but Shakespeare may have picked it up from Scot, *Discovery of Witchcraft* I.xviii, "Divine auguries were such, as . . . when trees spake, as before the death of Caesar."

123. *Auguries* omens; "Augures" (F) is probably a misprint. *understood relations* connections between incidents or objects that have been revealed, or properly interpreted, and so understood.

124. *By . . . rooks* by magpies and jackdaws (or crows) and rooks, all birds of ill omen (see III.ii.50–51 and note).

127–8. See III.vi.39–43. Macbeth has ceased telling his wife what he is doing.

132. *betimes* early in the morning.

133. *bent* determined.

By the worst means, the worst. For mine own good
135   All causes shall give way. I am in blood
Stepped in so far, that should I wade no more,
Returning were as tedious as go o'er.
Strange things I have in head that will to hand,
Which must be acted ere they may be scanned.

LADY MACBETH

140   You lack the season of all natures, sleep.

MACBETH

Come, we'll to sleep. My strange and self-abuse
Is the initiate fear that wants hard use;
We are yet but young in deed.

Exeunt.

Scene v: Thunder. Enter the three Witches, *meeting* HECATE.

FIRST WITCH

Why, how now, Hecate? You look angerly.

HECATE

Have I not reason, beldams as you are,
Saucy and overbold? How did you dare
To trade and traffic with Macbeth

---

135. *All . . . way*   i.e., all other affairs shall take second place.

139. *acted . . . scanned*   done first, examined later; see IV.i.145–7.

140. *season*   necessary period (of rest); or, possibly, preservative (seasoning).

141–2. *My . . . use*   i.e., my strange self-deception (in believing the Ghost of Banquo to be real) is the fear of a beginner not hardened by experience.

Scene v   This scene is regarded by many scholars as an interpolation by Middleton (see Introduction, p. xxii, and Appendix E). Hecate (pronounced as two syllables) is named at II.i.52 and III.ii.41.

2. *beldams*   old hags.

5 In riddles and affairs of death;
  And I, the mistress of your charms,
  The close contriver of all harms,
  Was never called to bear my part
  Or show the glory of our art?
10 And, which is worse, all you have done
  Hath been but for a wayward son,
  Spiteful and wrathful, who, as others do,
  Loves for his own ends, not for you.
  But make amends now: get you gone,
15 And at the pit of Acheron
  Meet me i' th' morning. Thither he
  Will come to know his destiny.
  Your vessels and your spells provide,
  Your charms, and every thing beside.
20 I am for th' air; this night I'll spend
  Unto a dismal and a fatal end.
  Great business must be wrought ere noon.
  Upon the corner of the moon
  There hangs a vap'rous drop profound;
25 I'll catch it ere it come to ground;
  And that distilled by magic sleights
  Shall raise such artificial sprites
  As by the strength of their illusion
  Shall draw him on to his confusion.
30 He shall spurn Fate, scorn death, and bear
  His hopes 'bove wisdom, grace, and fear;

---

7. *close* secret.
13. *Loves* i.e., loves evil.
15. *Acheron* i.e., Hell; properly, the name of a river in Hades.
21. *dismal* calamitous.
24. *profound* possessing hidden qualities.
27. *artificial* deceitful, cunning.
29. *confusion* ruin.

And you all know security
Is mortals' chiefest enemy.

Music and a song. Sing within, "Come
away, come away," etc.

Hark! I am called; my little spirit, see,
35   Sits in a foggy cloud and stays for me.

[*Exit* HECATE.]

FIRST WITCH

Come, let's make haste; she'll soon be back again.

Exeunt.

Scene vi: Enter LENNOX *and another* Lord.

LENNOX

My former speeches have but hit your thoughts,
Which can interpret farther; only I say

---

32. *security* overconfidence.

33. S.D. *"Come . . . away"* The text of a song beginning thus
appears in Middleton's *The Witch* III.iii (see Appendix E, p. 176); the
text is not appropriate here, and could hardly have been used in *Mac-*
beth as it is set forth in *The Witch*, where various characters from
Middleton's play are mentioned, and "a spirit like a cat" appears. In the
later and more elaborate productions of *Macbeth*, Hecate was apparently flown up to the "heavens" in a "cloud," or stage car, drawn by
pulleys.

Scene vi Macbeth went off in III.iv determined to see the Witches
"betimes," but Shakespeare postpones his meeting with them and
provides another quasi-choric scene similar to II.iv.; like the "Old
Man" of II.iv, the "Lord" here is anonymous. On a naturalistic time
scale, this scene could hardly intervene between III.iv and IV.i, but
time in the play does not go by the clock. The setting is somewhere in
Scotland, but the scene is not localized.

1. *hit* coincided with.

Things have been strangely borne. The gracious Duncan
Was pitied of Macbeth—marry, he was dead!
5 And the right valiant Banquo walked too late,
Whom you may say (if't please you) Fleance killed,
For Fleance fled. Men must not walk too late.
Who cannot want the thought, how monstrous
It was for Malcolm and for Donalbain
10 To kill their gracious father? Damnèd fact!
How it did grieve Macbeth! Did he not straight
In pious rage the two delinquents tear,
That were the slaves of drink and thralls of sleep?
Was not that nobly done? Ay, and wisely too;
15 For 'twould have angered any heart alive
To hear the men deny't. So that I say
He has borne all things well; and I do think
That, had he Duncan's sons under his key
(As, and't please Heaven, he shall not), they should find
20 What 'twere to kill a father; so should Fleance.
But peace! for from broad words, and 'cause he failed
His presence at the tyrant's feast, I hear
Macduff lives in disgrace. Sir, can you tell
Where he bestows himself?

---

3. *borne*   carried out, performed.

4. *of*   i.e., by.

8. *cannot want*   i.e., can lack; by enforcing his rhetoric with a double negative, Lennox says the opposite of what he apparently means. *monstrous*   pronounced as three syllables, "monstruous" (see Abbott, 477).

10. *fact*   evil deed, crime.

14–16. *Ay . . . deny't*   Lennox has changed his attitude since II.iii.95, where he thought the servants were guilty.

17. *borne*   managed, as at line 3 above.

19. *and't*   if it.

21. *from broad words*   on account of being outspoken.

21–2. *failed . . . presence*   did not appear (see III.iv.127–9).

24. *bestows himself*   lodges.

LORD

               The son of Duncan,

25 From whom this tyrant holds the due of birth,
Lives in the English court, and is received
Of the most pious Edward with such grace
That the malevolence of fortune nothing
Takes from his high respect. Thither Macduff
30 Is gone to pray the holy King upon his aid
To wake Northumberland and warlike Siward;
That, by the help of these (with Him above
To ratify the work) we may again
Give to our tables meat, sleep to our nights,
35 Free from our feasts and banquets bloody knives,
Do faithful homage and receive free honours,
All which we pine for now. And this report
Hath so exasperate the King that he
Prepares for some attempt of war.

LENNOX

               Sent he to Macduff?

---

25. *holds* i.e., withholds.

27. *Edward* Edward the Confessor, King of England 1042–66.

28–9. *That . . . respect* i.e., that in spite of the evil fortune (which has brought him into exile), Malcolm is held in high regard.

30. *upon his aid* on Malcolm's behalf.

31. *Siward* pronounced "Seward." The passage is based on Holinshed's statement: "Malcolm purchased such favour at King Edward's hands that old Siward, Earl of Northumberland, was appointed with ten thousand men to go with him into Scotland"; see IV.iii.189–92.

35. *Free . . . knives* i.e., rid our feasts and banquets of bloody knives.

36. *free* i.e., not paid for by servility to a tyrant.

38. *exasperate* i.e., exasperated; a fairly common form of past tense (Abbott, 341–2). *the* Hanmer's emendation of "their" (F). *King* i.e., Macbeth.

LORD

40 He did; and with an absolute "Sir, not I"
The cloudy messenger turns me his back,
And hums, as who should say, "You'll rue the time
That clogs me with this answer!"

LENNOX

And that well might
Advise him to a caution, t' hold what distance
45 His wisdom can provide. Some holy angel
Fly to the court of England and unfold
His message ere he come, that a swift blessing
May soon return to this our suffering country
Under a hand accursed!

LORD

I'll send my prayers with him.

Exeunt.

40—43. Compare III.iv.128—9.

41. *cloudy* sullen.

43. *clogs* hampers (by preventing me from fulfilling Macbeth's command).

44—5. *t' ... provide* i.e., to be cautious, and keep as far away from Macbeth as a sensible course of action will allow. Macduff's wife and children remain in Fife, and Lennox may have them in mind; see IV.ii.

49. *I'll ... him* referring back to line 30.

Act IV, scene i: Thunder. Enter the three Witches. [*A cauldron is mounted on-stage, with signs of fire and smoke.*]

FIRST WITCH

Thrice the brinded cat hath mewed.

SECOND WITCH

Thrice, and once the hedge-pig whined.

THIRD WITCH

Harpier cries; 'tis time, 'tis time.

FIRST WITCH

Round about the cauldron go;
5   In the poisoned entrails throw—
Toad, that under cold stone
Days and nights has thirty-one

---

scene i The scene is not localized. But at III.v.15, Hecate talks of "the pit of Acheron" as their meeting place, and see line 46 of this scene. The Witches meet at night (see line 47). The cauldron, with signs of fire and smoke, apparently made quite a sensation: Ben Jonson had a "Hell" setting in *The Masque of Queens* (1609), with flame, smoke, and twelve witches, and Middleton used a cauldron for a scene (V.ii) in *The Witch* (?1610). It is not clear exactly how this scene was staged at the Globe, although smoke was easy enough to make by burning resin. Probably the cauldron was mounted over a trap door, and the Apparitions, coming on-stage through the trap, appeared to rise from the cauldron.

1. *brinded* brindled, tabby; the First Witch's familiar is a cat (see I.i.8).

2. *hedge-pig* hedgehog; her familiar was a toad in I.i., but the toad has another use here (see line 6).

3. *Harpier* the name of her familiar (perhaps derived from the classical Harpies, who were ministers of vengeance).

4. *Round . . . go* Probably the First Witch moves around the cauldron by herself; and see line 10 and note.

Sweltered venom sleeping got,
Boil thou first i' th' charmèd pot.

ALL

10   Double, double, toil and trouble;
Fire burn, and cauldron bubble.

SECOND WITCH

Fillet of a fenny snake,
In the cauldron boil and bake;
Eye of newt, and toe of frog,
15   Wool of bat, and tongue of dog;
Adder's fork, and blindworm's sting,
Lizard's leg, and owlet's wing;
For a charm of powerful trouble,
Like a Hell-broth boil and bubble.

ALL

20   Double, double, toil and trouble;
Fire burn, and cauldron bubble.

THIRD WITCH

Scale of dragon, tooth of wolf,
Witches' mummy, maw and gulf

6—8. In *News from Scotland* (1591), Agnes Sampson, intending to
kill King James, "took a black toad, and did hang up the same by the
heels, three days, and collected and gathered the venom as it dropped";
see Introduction, pp. xiv—xv.

8. *Sweltered*   exuded like sweat (in its sleep). The charm is designed to double strife and sorrow among their victims (see line 18);
but "double" may also mean "turn about" and all move about the
cauldron here.

12. *Fillet . . . snake*   slice of a snake from the fens.

16. *fork*   double tongue. *blindworm's sting*   The blindworm is a
harmless kind of legless lizard, but—like other creatures in the Witches'
list—was then thought to be venomous.

23. *mummy*   mummified flesh, believed to have potency as a drug.
maw and gulf   throat and belly, both implying voracious appetite.

Of the ravened salt-sea shark;
25   Root of hemlock digged i' th' dark;
Liver of blaspheming Jew,
Gall of goat, and slips of yew
Slivered in the moon's eclipse;
Nose of Turk and Tartar's lips;
30   Finger of birth-strangled babe
Ditch-delivered by a drab,
Make the gruel thick and slab.
Add thereto a tiger's chaudron,
For th' ingredients of our cauldron.

ALL

35   Double, double, toil and trouble;
Fire burn, and cauldron bubble.

SECOND WITCH

Cool it with a baboon's blood;
Then the charm is firm and good.

Enter HECATE *and the other three* Witches.

---

24. *ravened*   glutted with prey; an odd use of the verb "raven" meaning "to devour."

25. *i' th' dark*   when its poison was thought to be most potent.

27. *yew*   then believed to be poisonous.

28. *Slivered*   stripped or cut off. *eclipse*   an especially ominous and unlucky time, and so appropriate for evil schemes.

29. *Turk . . . lips*   Turks and Tartars were thought to be savagely cruel, and, as pagans, being unchristened—like the "Jew" (line 26) and "babe" (line 30)—they are valued by the Witches, who oppose Christianity (see lines 51–2).

31. *drab*   prostitute.

32. *slab*   dense.

33. *chaudron*   entrails.

37. *baboon's*   accented on the first syllable.

39–43. If III.v. is an interpolation, then these lines must be too. Hecate has no function in the scene; the "other three Witches" in the stage directions are superfluous; "elves and fairies" (line 42) are in-

HECATE

O well done! I commend your pains,
40 And every one shall share i' th' gains.
And now about the cauldron sing,
Like elves and fairies in a ring,
Enchanting all that you put in.

> *Music and a song. "Black spirits," etc.*
> > [*Exeunt* HECATE *and the other three* Witches.]

SECOND WITCH

By the pricking of my thumbs,
45 Something wicked this way comes.—   [*Knocking.*]
Open, locks, whoever knocks.

> *Enter* MACBETH.

MACBETH

How now, you secret, black, and midnight hags?
What is't you do?

ALL

A deed without a name.

MACBETH

I conjure you, by that which you profess—
50 Howe'er you come to know it—answer me:

---

appropriate here. The text of the song "Black spirits and white" appears in Middleton's *The Witch* (V.ii), but there involves a character called Firestone, Hecate's son. See III.v.33 and note, and Appendix E.

43. S.D. *Exeunt*   No "Exeunt" is marked for Hecate and the extra Witches in F.

46. The line indicates that knocking is heard, although there is no specific direction for it in F. A barrier or door that opens mysteriously to let Macbeth into the Witches' secret gathering would seem appropriate here. Lennox apparently stands guard outside the door, to enter on Macbeth's call at line 134.

49. *that . . . profess*   i.e., the art of black magic.

Though you untie the winds and let them fight
Against the churches; though the yeasty waves
Confound and swallow navigation up;
Though bladed corn be lodged and trees blown down;
55   Though castles topple on their warders' heads;
Though palaces and pyramids do slope
Their heads to their foundations; though the treasure
Of nature's germens tumble all together,
Even till destruction sicken—answer me
To what I ask you.

FIRST WITCH

Speak.

SECOND WITCH

Demand.

THIRD WITCH

60   We'll answer.

FIRST WITCH

Say if th' hadst rather hear it from our mouths,
Or from our masters?

MACBETH

Call 'em; let me see 'em.

---

51. *winds*   See I.iii.11–15.

52. *yeasty*   frothing.

54. *bladed . . . lodged*   i.e., young corn (in the leaf or blade), not yet in the ear and so unlikely to be "lodged," or beaten flat by rain or wind.

58. *germens*   seeds or rudiments from which it was thought all living organisms developed (see *Lear* III.ii.8–9. and *Winter's Tale* IV.iv.470–1); Theobald's emendation of "Germaine" (F).

59. *sicken*   i.e., through surfeit.

61. *th'*   thou.

62. *masters*   presumably the evil spirits who take the shape of the Apparitions.

FIRST WITCH

Pour in sow's blood, that hath eaten
Her nine farrow; grease, that's sweaten
65 From the murderer's gibbet, throw
Into the flame.

ALL

Come high or low;
Thy self and office deftly show.

Thunder. First Apparition, *an armed head.*

MACBETH

Tell me, thou unknown power—

FIRST WITCH

                     He knows thy thought:
Hear his speech, but say thou nought.

FIRST APPARITION

70 Macbeth! Macbeth! Macbeth! beware Macduff;
Beware the Thane of Fife. Dismiss me. Enough.

He descends.

MACBETH

Whate'er thou art, for thy good caution, thanks;
Thou hast harped my fear aright. But one word more—

FIRST WITCH

He will not be commanded. Here's another,
75 More potent than the first.

Thunder. Second Apparition, *a bloody child.*

---

64. *nine farrow*　her litter of nine piglets.

67. S.D. *armed head*　perhaps representing Macduff, but more probably reflecting Macbeth himself, whose armed head is cut off and brought on-stage by Macduff at V.viii. 19.

73. *harped*　struck the note of.

75. S.D. *bloody child*　The Second Apparition suggests Macduff, "from his mother's womb / Untimely ripped" (see V.vii.44–5).

SECOND APPARITION

Macbeth! Macbeth! Macbeth!

MACBETH

Had I three ears, I'd hear thee.

SECOND APPARITION

Be bloody, bold, and resolute; laugh to scorn
The power of man; for none of woman born
80 Shall harm Macbeth.

Descends.

MACBETH

Then live, Macduff; what need I fear of thee?
But yet I'll make assurance double sure,
And take a bond of Fate: thou shalt not live,
That I may tell pale-hearted fear it lies,
And sleep in spite of thunder.

*Thunder. Third Apparition, a child crowned,
with a tree in his hand.*

85   What is this
That rises like the issue of a king,
And wears upon his baby-brow the round
And top of sovereignty?

79—81. Holinshed says only, "a certain witch, whom he had in great trust, had told that he should never be slain with man born of any woman, nor vanquished till the wood of Birnam came to the castle of Dunsinane" (see Appendix B, p. 166).

80. The short line provides for a pause before Macbeth speaks.

83. *take . . . live* i.e., by killing Macduff, he will bind Fate to carry out the pledge made by the Apparition.

85. S.D. *child . . . hand* symbolizing Malcolm; the tree is an allusion to the boughs cut from Birnam Wood that Malcolm has his soldiers carry (see V.iv.3—7).

88. *top* i.e., the crown, as the summit of his ambitious aspirations.

ALL

Listen, but speak not to't.

THIRD APPARITION

Be lion-mettled, proud, and take no care
90 Who chafes, who frets, or where conspirers are.
Macbeth shall never vanquished be until
Great Birnam Wood to high Dunsinane Hill
Shall come against him.

Descends.

MACBETH

That will never be:
Who can impress the forest, bid the tree
95 Unfix his earth-bound root? Sweet bodements! good!
Rebellious head, rise never till the Wood
Of Birnam rise, and our high-placed Macbeth
Shall live the lease of nature, pay his breath
To time and mortal custom. Yet my heart

91–3. *Macbeth . . . him* See note to lines 79–81 above.

93. S.D. *Descends* "Descend" in F, where directions are often imperative; in this scene, however, F has "Descends" at lines 71 and 80.

93–100. Note how Macbeth speaks here in rhyme, continuing the pattern used by the Witches and Apparitions. Some scholars have thought lines 93–9 should be assigned to the First Witch.

94. *impress* compel into service.

95. *bodements* omens.

96. *head* Theobald's emendation of "dead" (F) is generally accepted as fitting in with "conspirers" (line 90); the word "head" here means "armed force" (as at *1 Henry IV*, I.iii.284), and is appropriate to the action, since Malcolm is already raising a force against Macbeth (III.vi.29–31). It has been argued, however, that "dead" refers to Banquo's Ghost, so soon to rise again, at line 110.

96–7. *rise . . . rise* Shakespeare is not likely to have repeated "rise" in this line and the next, which suggests some corruption of the text here.

98. *lease of nature* normal span of life.

100 Throbs to know one thing: tell me, if your art
     Can tell so much, shall Banquo's issue ever
     Reign in this kingdom?

                         ALL
              Seek to know no more.

                       MACBETH
     I will be satisfied. Deny me this,
     And an eternal curse fall on you! Let me know.—
105 Why sinks that cauldron? and what noise is this?

                                              Oboes.

                    FIRST WITCH
     Show!

                    SECOND WITCH
     Show!

                    THIRD WITCH
     Show!

                         ALL
     Show his eyes, and grieve his heart;
110 Come like shadows, so depart.

          A show of eight Kings, *and* BANQUO; *last* [King] *with a*
                      glass in his hand.

---

    105. *sinks that cauldron* apparently lowered through a trap door.
noise music, as at *Tempest* III.ii.130.

    110. S.D. *and . . . hand* In F the S.D. ends, "Banquo last, with a
glass in his hand," which contradicts the text, lines 118–23; editors
have generally altered the direction to agree with Macbeth's words.
The "show" was designed to compliment King James I of England
(James VI of Scotland), for the Stuarts claimed descent from Banquo
and James I was the ninth Stuart monarch. The eighth was his mother,
Mary, Queen of Scots, and scholars have wondered whether Shake-

MACBETH

Thou art too like the spirit of Banquo. Down!
Thy crown does sear mine eyeballs. And thy hair,
Thou other gold-bound brow, is like the first.
A third is like the former.—Filthy hags!

115 Why do you show me this?—A fourth? Start, eyes!
What, will the line stretch out to th' crack of doom?
Another yet? A seventh?—I'll see no more—
And yet the eighth appears, who bears a glass
Which shows me many more; and some I see

120 That twofold balls and treble scepters carry.
Horrible sight! Now, I see, 'tis true,
For the blood-boltered Banquo smiles upon me
And points at them for his.—

                              [Apparitions *vanish*.]
                         What? is this so?

---

speare intended her to appear; the direction, however, specifies
"Kings," and in any case a procession of ghostly crowned figures would
sufficiently carry the compliment. The "glass," or mirror, of line 118
shows many descendants carrying on the line of James I. See H.N. Paul,
The Royal Play of Macbeth.

118. *glass* magic mirror, in which the future could be seen.

120. *twofold . . . scepters* The "balls" are probably the orbs carried by James when crowned in Scotland and then in England; "treble
scepters" may refer to the single scepter carried in the Scottish coronation and the two carried in the English coronation. In any case, the
passage points to the union of Great Britain under King James. See
E.K. Chambers, *William Shakespeare*, I, 473.

122. *blood-boltered* his hair clotted with blood.

FIRST WITCH

Ay, sir, all this is so. But why
125   Stands Macbeth thus amazedly?
Come, sisters, cheer we up his sprites
And show the best of our delights.
I'll charm the air to give a sound
While you perform your antic round,
130   That this great King may kindly say,
Our duties did his welcome pay.

Music. The Witches *dance, and vanish.*

MACBETH

Where are they? Gone? Let this pernicious hour
Stand aye accursèd in the calendar!—
Come in, without there!

Enter LENNOX

LENNOX

What's your grace's will?

MACBETH

Saw you the Weird Sisters?

LENNOX

135   No, my lord.

MACBETH

Came they not by you?

124—31. These lines are regarded by many critics as an interpolation, spoiling what could be a notable theatrical effect as Macbeth turns from the show of Kings to find the Witches vanished; but the passage is effective in its own way, and lines 130—31 are nicely ironical in relation to Macbeth's "welcome" at line 47 above; see Appendix E, p. 176.

129. *antic round*   fantastic dance.

134. *Come . . . Enter* LENNOX   See line 46 and note.

LENNOX

No indeed, my lord.

MACBETH

Infected be the air whereon they ride,
And damned all those that trust them! I did hear
The galloping of horse. Who was't came by?

LENNOX

140 'Tis two or three, my lord, that bring you word
Macduff is fled to England.

MACBETH

Fled to England?

LENNOX

Ay, my good lord.

MACBETH

[*Aside*] Time, thou anticipat'st my dread exploits;
The flighty purpose never is o'ertook
145 Unless the deed go with it. From this moment
The very firstlings of my heart shall be
The firstlings of my hand. And even now,
To crown my thoughts with acts, be it thought and done:
The castle of Macduff I will surprise,
150 Seize upon Fife, give to th' edge o' th' sword
His wife, his babes, and all unfortunate souls

---

138. *damned . . . them* including himself.

142. Another short line (see line 80 above and note) giving Macbeth time to gather his thoughts as he turns aside.

143. *anticipat'st* forestalls.

144—5. *The . . . it* The image is of "purpose" fleeing swiftly ("flighty"), and never being caught up with; the idea is that we never carry out our purpose unless we act at once.

146. *firstlings* first motions (properly, first products of).

That trace him in his line. No boasting like a fool,
This deed I'll do before this purpose cool;
But no more sights! [*To* LENNOX] Where are these gentlemen?
155 Come, bring me where they are.

                                      Exeunt.

Scene ii: Enter Macduff's Wife, *her* Son, *and* ROSS.

LADY MACDUFF

What had he done to make him fly the land?

ROSS

You must have patience, madam.

LADY MACDUFF

                             He had none;
His flight was madness. When our actions do not,
Our fears do make us traitors.

ROSS

                             You know not
5 Whether it was his wisdom or his fear.

LADY MACDUFF

Wisdom? To leave his wife, to leave his babes,
His mansion, and his titles, in a place

---

152. *trace him* succeed him, are related to him.

Scene ii Macbeth's determination to act instantly is brought home
by this immediate transfer of scene to Macduff's castle in Fife. The idea
for the scene stems from Holinshed, who says that Macbeth besieged
Macduff's castle and, when the gates were opened to him, had Lady
Macduff and her children killed (see Appendix B, p. 166). Shakespeare
invented Ross's visit and the dialogue between mother and son.

3–5. *madness . . . wisdom* See III.vi.44–5, where Lennox thought
it "wisdom" for Macduff to keep far away from Macbeth.

7. *titles* legal rights; i.e., his possessions and rents.

From whence himself does fly? He loves us not,
He wants the natural touch. For the poor wren,
10   The most diminutive of birds, will fight,
Her young ones in her nest, against the owl.
All is the fear and nothing is the love;
As little is the wisdom, where the flight
So runs against all reason.

ROSS

         My dearest coz,
15   I pray you school yourself. But for your husband,
He is noble, wise, judicious, and best knows
The fits o' th' season. I dare not speak much further;
But cruel are the times, when we are traitors
And do not know ourselves; when we hold rumour
20   From what we fear, yet know not what we fear,
But float upon a wild and violent sea
Each way, and move—I take my leave of you;
Shall not be long but I'll be here again.

---

9. *wants . . . touch*   i.e., lacks natural affection for his family.

9–11. *For . . . owl*   A fine image, although the wren does not in fact behave in this way.

12. Compare I John 4:18, "There is no fear in love; but perfect love casteth out fear."

14. *coz*   short for "cousin," but used generally as a familiar term of address.

15. *school*   control.

17. *fits*   disorders, as at *Coriolanus* III.ii.33.

19. *do . . . ourselves*   i.e., do not know that we are traitors.

19–20. *when . . . From what we fear*   i.e., when we are led by our fear to trust all kinds of rumors.

21–2. *float . . . move*   i.e., float, moving this way and that as the waves toss but making no headway, in a sea of uncertainty.

23. *Shall*   i.e., it shall.

Things at the worst will cease, or else climb upward
25　To what they were before. My pretty cousin,
Blessing upon you!

LADY MACDUFF

Fathered he is, and yet he's fatherless.

ROSS

I am so much a fool, should I stay longer,
It would be my disgrace and your discomfort:
I take my leave at once.

Exit ROSS.

LADY MACDUFF

30　　　　　　　　　　Sirrah, your father's dead;
And what will you do now? How will you live?

SON

As birds do, mother.

LADY MACDUFF

What, with worms and flies?

SON

With what I get, I mean; and so do they.

24–5. *Things . . . before*　a vague and gloomy forecast, suggesting at the worst a cessation that could be the oblivion of death, and at the best a return to some earlier condition.

28–9. *I am . . . discomfort*　i.e., my sympathy undermines my self-control to such an extent that if I were to stay longer, I should disgrace myself by weeping and distress you.

30. *Sirrah*　sometimes used as a familiar term of address by parents to children.

32. *As birds do*　See Matthew 6:26, "Behold the fowls of the air: . . . Your heavenly Father feedeth them."

LADY MACDUFF

Poor bird! thou'dst never fear the net nor lime,
The pitfall nor the gin.

SON

35   Why should I, mother?
Poor birds they are not set for.
My father is not dead, for all your saying.

LADY MACDUFF

Yes, he is dead. How wilt thou do for a father?

SON

Nay, how will you do for a husband?

LADY MACDUFF

40 Why, I can buy me twenty at any market.

SON

Then you'll buy 'em to sell again.

LADY MACDUFF

Thou speak'st with all thy wit;
And yet, i' faith, with wit enough for thee.

SON

Was my father a traitor, mother?

LADY MACDUFF

45 Ay, that he was.

SON

What is a traitor?

---

34. *lime*   birdlime.
35. *gin*   snare.
36. Traps are not set for "poor" birds (only for fat, or rich, ones).
The son pauses after the short line before speaking again of his father.
44. *traitor*   He is thinking of lines 4—18 above.

LADY MACDUFF

Why, one that swears and lies.

SON

And be all traitors that do so?

LADY MACDUFF

Every one that does so is a traitor, and must be hanged.

SON

50 And must they all be hanged that swear and lie?

LADY MACDUFF

Every one.

SON

Who must hang them?

LADY MACDUFF

Why, the honest men.

SON

55 Then the liars and swearers are fools, for there are liars and
swearers enough to beat the honest men and hang up them.

LADY MACDUFF

Now God help thee, poor monkey! But how wilt thou do for
a father?

SON

If he were dead, you'ld weep for him. If you would not, it were
60 a good sign that I should quickly have a new father.

LADY MACDUFF

Poor prattler, how thou talk'st!

---

47. *swears and lies* i.e., takes an oath (as of allegiance, or to love
his wife) and is false to it. This exchange recalls the Porter's talk of
equivocation in II.iii, and some have seen here another allusion to the
Jesuit Henry Garnet; see II.iii.7—9 and note.

Enter a Messenger.

MESSENGER

Bless you, fair dame! I am not to you known,
Though in your state of honour I am perfect.
65 I doubt some danger does approach you nearly.
If you will take a homely man's advice,
Be not found here; hence, with your little ones.
To fright you thus methinks I am too savage;
To do worse to you were fell cruelty,
70 Which is too nigh your person. Heaven preserve you!
I dare abide no longer.

                                             Exit.

LADY MACDUFF

                  Whither should I fly?
I have done no harm. But I remember now
I am in this earthly world, where to do harm
Is often laudable, to do good sometime
75 Accounted dangerous folly. Why then, alas,
Do I put up that womanly defence,
To say I have done no harm?—What are these faces?

Enter Murderers.

MURDERER

Where is your husband?

LADY MACDUFF

I hope in no place so unsanctified
Where such as thou mayst find him.

---

64. *in . . . perfect* i.e., I know perfectly well what high rank you
hold. He is apologizing for rushing so abruptly into her presence.
65. *doubt* fear.
68. *thus methinks* so printed in F2; F reads "thus. Me thinkes"
69. *do worse* i.e., by telling her in more detail what the danger is.

MURDERER

80   He's a traitor.

SON

Thou liest, thou shag-haired villain.

MURDERER

What, you egg!

Young fry of treachery!   [*Stabbing him.*]

SON

He has killed me, mother.

Run away, I pray you!   [*Dies.*]

Exit [LADY MACDUFF] *crying "Murder!"*
[*and pursued by the* Murderers].

Scene iii: Enter MALCOLM *and* MACDUFF.

MALCOLM

Let us seek out some desolate shade, and there
Weep our sad bosoms empty.

---

81. *shag-haired* This emendation of "shagge-ear'd" (F) was suggested in 1793 by George Steevens, and has been widely accepted ("hear" was a common Elizabethan spelling of "hair," and the printer may simply have omitted the *h*). Shaggy or unkempt hair was the mark of a ruffian.

Scene iii At the English court of Edward the Confessor. This scene establishes the idea of a good king to set against Macbeth—and links Malcolm with the saintly Edward; it is the one scene that takes us outside Scotland. The discussion between Malcolm and Macduff on kingship (lines 1–137) is largely borrowed from Holinshed, where it forms the only extended piece of dialogue in his account of Macbeth (see Appendix B, p. 167). Between scenes ii and iii Ross has traveled from Fife to England.

MACDUFF

　　　　　Let us rather
Hold fast the mortal sword, and like good men
Bestride our downfall'n birthdom. Each new morn
5　New widows howl, new orphans cry, new sorrows
Strike Heaven on the face, that it resounds
As if it felt with Scotland and yelled out
Like syllable of dolour.

MALCOLM

　　　　　What I believe I'll wail;
What know, believe; and what I can redress,
10　As I shall find the time to friend, I will.
What you have spoke, it may be so perchance.
This tyrant, whose sole name blisters our tongues,
Was once thought honest; you have loved him well,
He hath not touched you yet. I am young, but something
15　You may discern of him through me, and wisdom
To offer up a weak, poor, innocent lamb
T' appease an angry god.

MACDUFF

I am not treacherous.

---

3. *mortal*　death-dealing.

4. *Bestride*　i.e., defend. *downfall'n*　F has "downfall," then a proper form of the past participle. *birthdom*　i.e., fatherland.

6. *that*　so that.

8. *wail*　bewail, grieve for.

10. *to friend*　i.e., friendly, favorable.

12. *sole*　mere.

13. *honest*　virtuous.

14—16. *something . . . lamb*　i.e., you may see something of him in me (he was thought virtuous when young, and I may become like him), and may see too that it would be wisdom to betray me to him. Many editors follow Theobald in emending "discerne" (F) to "deserve."

MALCOLM

But Macbeth is.
A good and virtuous nature may recoil
20   In an imperial charge. But I shall crave your pardon:
That which you are my thoughts cannot transpose;
Angels are bright still, though the brightest fell.
Though all things foul would wear the brows of grace,
Yet grace must still look so.

MACDUFF

I have lost my hopes.

MALCOLM

25   Perchance even there where I did find my doubts.
Why in that rawness left you wife and child,
Those precious motives, those strong knots of love,
Without leave-taking?—I pray you,
Let not my jealousies be your dishonours,
30   But mine own safeties. You may be rightly just,
Whatever I shall think.

MACDUFF

Bleed, bleed, poor country!
Great tyranny, lay thou thy basis sure,

19—20. *recoil . . . charge*   give way to a royal command.

21. *That . . . transpose*   i.e., my thoughts cannot change what you are; see lines 30—31.

22. See Isaiah 14:12, "How art thou fallen from heaven, O Lucifer, thou fair morning child," and Revelation 9:1.

23, 24. *grace*   holiness, as at line 159.

24. *so*   i.e., like itself.

25. *there*   i.e., in Macduff's leaving Scotland.

26. *rawness*   unprotected state.

27. *motives*   reasons (for staying in Scotland).

28. A short line, suggesting a pause after "leave-taking."

29. *jealousies*   suspicions.

For goodness dare not check thee! Wear thou thy wrongs,
The title is affeered! Fare thee well, lord;
35   I would not be the villain that thou think'st
For the whole space that's in the tyrant's grasp,
And the rich East to boot.

MALCOLM

         Be not offended;
I speak not as in absolute fear of you.
I think our country sinks beneath the yoke;
40   It weeps, it bleeds, and each new day a gash
Is added to her wounds. I think withal
There would be hands uplifted in my right;
And here from gracious England have I offer
Of goodly thousands. But, for all this,
45   When I shall tread upon the tyrant's head,
Or wear it on my sword, yet my poor country
Shall have more vices than it had before,
More suffer, and more sundry ways than ever,
By him that shall succeed.

MACDUFF

         What should he be?

MALCOLM

50   It is myself I mean; in whom I know
All the particulars of vice so grafted
That, when they shall be opened, black Macbeth
Will seem as pure as snow, and the poor state

---

33. *goodness . . . thee*   criticizing Malcolm's fear (see line 38).

34. *affeered*   confirmed; properly a term meaning to fix the amount of a fine.

43. *gracious England*   i.e., the holy King Edward the Confessor, who reigned 1042–66.

52. *opened*   revealed; but suggesting buds opening, after "grafted."

Esteem him as a lamb, being compared
With my confineless harms.

MACDUFF

55   Not in the legions
Of horrid Hell can come a devil more damned
In evils to top Macbeth.

MALCOLM

                    I grant him bloody,
Luxurious, avaricious, false, deceitful,
Sudden, malicious, smacking of every sin
60   That has a name. But there's no bottom, none,
In my voluptuousness: your wives, your daughters,
Your matrons, and your maids could not fill up
The cistern of my lust; and my desire
All continent impediments would o'erbear
65   That did oppose my will. Better Macbeth
Than such an one to reign.

MACDUFF

                    Boundless intemperance
In nature is a tyranny; it hath been
Th' untimely emptying of the happy throne
And fall of many kings. But fear not yet

---

55. *confineless*   boundless.

58. *Luxurious*   lecherous, a common meaning at this time. Macbeth, however, is not actually shown as lustful in the play, and in Holinshed Malcolm says only that his own "immoderate lust" would be worse than Macbeth's "bloody tyranny."

59. *Sudden*   i.e., given to unpremeditated violence.

64. *continent*   restraining (punning on the alternative meaning "chaste").

66–7. *Boundless . . . tyranny*   i.e., in the little kingdom of man's nature, it is a tyranny when sensual appetites take over the rule that should be exercised by reason; compare *Caesar* II.i.67–9.

70 To take upon you what is yours; you may
    Convey your pleasures in a spacious plenty
    And yet seem cold, the time you may so hoodwink;
    We have willing dames enough. There cannot be
    That vulture in you, to devour so many
75 As will to greatness dedicate themselves,
    Finding it so inclined.

MALCOLM

                With this there grows
    In my most ill-composed affection such
    A stanchless avarice that, were I King,
    I should cut off the nobles for their lands,
80 Desire his jewels and this other's house;
    And my more-having would be as a sauce
    To make me hunger more, that I should forge
    Quarrels unjust against the good and loyal,
    Destroying them for wealth.

MACDUFF

                This avarice
85 Sticks deeper, grows with more pernicious root

---

71. *Convey* manage secretly; the word is taken from Holinshed (see Appendix B, p. 167), but the meaning was common.

72. *cold, . . . hoodwink* the punctuation proposed by Theobald; F has a full stop after "cold." For the sense here, see I.v.61–2 and note.

77. *ill-composed affection* disposition made up of evil.

78. *stanchless* insatiable.

79. *cut off* put to death, as at I Samuel 20:15 (*Authorized Version*), "when the Lord hath cut off the enemies of David."

80. *his* i.e., one man's.

82. *that* so that.

Than summer-seeming lust, and it hath been
The sword of our slain kings; yet do not fear,
Scotland hath foisons to fill up your will
Of your mere own. All these are portable,
90   With other graces weighed.

MALCOLM

But I have none. The king-becoming graces,
As justice, verity, temp'rance, stableness,
Bounty, perseverance, mercy, lowliness,
Devotion, patience, courage, fortitude,
95   I have no relish of them, but abound
In the division of each several crime,
Acting it many ways. Nay, had I power, I should
Pour the sweet milk of concord into Hell,
Uproar the universal peace, confound
All unity on earth.

MACDUFF

100   O Scotland, Scotland!

---

86. *summer-seeming*   transitory, like summer. Lust dies with old age (or winter), but avarice does not.

86—7. *it . . . kings*   from Holinshed, where Macduff says, "for that crime [avarice] the most part of our kings have been slain" (see Appendix B, p. 168).

88—9. *foisons . . . own*   i.e., plenty to supply your appetite out of your very own property (meaning the royal domains).

89. *portable*   endurable.

90. *With . . . weighed*   balanced against other virtues.

93. *perseverance*   accented on the second syllable.

95. *relish*   trace.

96. *division*   variation, or descant, as in music.

97—100. *Nay . . . earth*   This has no counterpart in Holinshed, and Dover Wilson thinks that the lines allude to James I's desire to be the maker of a universal peace; see Introduction, p. xvi. The image fits what Macbeth has done, rather than what Malcolm might conceivably do.

98. *milk of concord*   Compare I.v.15 and note.

99. *Uproar*   throw into confusion.

MALCOLM

If such a one be fit to govern, speak:
I am as I have spoken.

MACDUFF

Fit to govern?
No, not to live. O nation miserable!
With an untitled tyrant, bloody-sceptered,
105 When shalt thou see thy wholesome days again?
Since that the truest issue of thy throne
By his own interdiction stands accused,
And does blaspheme his breed! Thy royal father
Was a most sainted king; the queen that bore thee,
110 Oft'ner upon her knees than on her feet,
Died every day she lived. Fare thee well!
These evils thou repeat'st upon thyself
Hath banished me from Scotland. O my breast,
Thy hope ends here!

MALCOLM

Macduff, this noble passion,
115 Child of integrity, hath from my soul
Wiped the black scruples, reconciled my thoughts
To thy good truth and honour. Devilish Macbeth

---

104. *untitled*   having no right to rule.

107. *interdiction*   in Scottish law, a "restraint imposed upon a person incapable of managing his own affairs" (OED); Malcolm has announced his unfitness to govern, and has put a restraint upon himself.

108. *blaspheme*   abuse.

111. *Died . . . lived*   See I Corinthians 15:31, "by our rejoicing which I have in Christ Jesu our Lord, I die daily."

112. *repeat'st upon*   recite against; "repeat" commonly meant "say" with no idea of repetition.

113. *Hath*   i.e., have (see I.iii.148 and note).

116. *black scruples*   i.e., the evil doubts I had about you.

By many of these trains hath sought to win me
Into his power, and modest wisdom plucks me
120   From overcredulous haste; but God above
Deal between thee and me! For even now
I put myself to thy direction and
Unspeak mine own detraction; here abjure
The taints and blames I laid upon myself
125   For strangers to my nature. I am yet
Unknown to woman, never was forsworn,
Scarcely have coveted what was mine own,
At no time broke my faith, would not betray
The Devil to his fellow, and delight
130   No less in truth than life. My first false speaking
Was this upon myself. What I am truly
Is thine and my poor country's to command;
Whither indeed, before thy here-approach,
Old Siward, with ten thousand warlike men,
135   Already at a point, was setting forth.
Now we'll together, and the chance of goodness
Be like our warranted quarrel! Why are you silent?

---

118. *trains*   stratagems, or snares.

119. *modest wisdom*   i.e., sober judgment.

123. *mine own detraction*   my defamation of myself.

125. *For*   as being.

134. *Old Siward*   Earl of Northumberland, as Holinshed describes him (see Appendix B, p. 169).

135. *at a point*   prepared, equipped; see *Lear* I.iv.325.

136. *we'll together*   i.e., we will march together.

136–7. *the . . . quarrel*   i.e., may the chance of success accord with the justice of our cause! "Goodness" here seems to mean "good fortune"; "quarrel" = "ground of complaint or hostile action" (see line 83). However, the phrase is difficult, and the explanation here given has not satisfied all critics, though none has suggested a better one.

MACDUFF

Such welcome and unwelcome things at once
'Tis hard to reconcile.

Enter a Doctor.

MALCOLM

140   Well, more anon. Comes the King forth, I pray you?

DOCTOR

Ay, sir; there are a crew of wretched souls
That stay his cure; their malady convinces
The great assay of art. But, at his touch,
Such sanctity hath Heaven given his hand,
They presently amend.

MALCOLM

145   I thank you, doctor.

Exit [Doctor].

MACDUFF

What's the disease he means?

MALCOLM

              'Tis called the Evil.
A most miraculous work in this good King,
Which often, since my here-remain in England,

140—59. This account of a good king is elaborated from Holinshed's description of Edward in his *Chronicles of England* (see Appendix B, p. 170), but with additions referring to practices of Shakespeare's own time (see lines 153—4 and note). A compliment to James I is probably intended (see line 146 and note).

142. *stay his cure* wait for him to cure them.

142—3. *convinces . . . art* i.e., defeats the best efforts of science.

146. *the Evil* "The King's Evil," or scrofula, was thought to be curable at the touch of any king descended from Edward the Confessor, and the practice was continued by James I, who is perhaps being complimented in the account of "this good King."

148. *here-remain* stay; compare "here-approach," line 133.

I have seen him do. How he solicits Heaven,
150   Himself best knows; but strangely-visited people,
All swollen and ulcerous, pitiful to the eye,
The mere despair of surgery, he cures,
Hanging a golden stamp about their necks,
Put on with holy prayers; and 'tis spoken,
155   To the succeeding royalty he leaves
The healing benediction. With this strange virtue,
He hath a heavenly gift of prophecy,
And sundry blessings hang about his throne
That speak him full of grace.

Enter ROSS.

MACDUFF
See who comes here.

MALCOLM
160   My countryman; but yet I know him not.

MACDUFF
My ever gentle cousin, welcome hither.

---

150. *strangely-visited*   strangely afflicted (visited with the disease).

152. *mere*   absolute.

153–4. *Hanging . . . prayers*   A gold coin was presented to each of the sufferers at a special service, instituted by Henry VII (reigned 1485–1509) and added to the *Book of Common Prayer* in the late seventeenth century.

154. *'tis spoken*   i.e., it is said.

156. *virtue*   healing power; so used in the Bible, as at Luke 6:19.

159–240. The rest of the scene is Shakespeare's invention, and no hint for it is provided by Holinshed.

160. *My . . . not*   Malcolm presumably recognizes his dress, but just what marked Ross as a Scotsman is not known. Macduff wears a hat (see line 208), which might be the distinguishing feature; in *1 Henry IV*, II.iv.348, Scotsmen are called "blue-caps."

MALCOLM

I know him now. Good God, betimes remove
The means that makes us strangers!

ROSS

                 Sir, amen.

MACDUFF

Stands Scotland where it did?

ROSS

              Alas, poor country,
165   Almost afraid to know itself! It cannot
Be called our mother, but our grave; where nothing,
But who knows nothing, is once seen to smile;
Where sighs and groans and shrieks that rent the air
Are made, not marked; where violent sorrow seems
170   A modern ecstasy. The dead man's knell
Is there scarce asked for who, and good men's lives
Expire before the flowers in their caps,
Dying or ere they sicken.

MACDUFF

              O relation
Too nice, and yet too true!

---

163. *means* condition; often used in the plural with a singular sense and construction.

167. *once* ever.

168. *rent* i.e., rend; a common early form of the verb.

170. *modern ecstasy* commonplace disorder of the mind. This is the usual sense of "modern" in Shakespeare, as at *All's Well* II.iii.3; for "ecstasy," see *Macbeth* III.ii.22.

173. *or ere* before ever; "or" in this phrase means "before," and is the same word as "ere," but the emphatic "or e'er" ("or ever") gradually came to be used by poets simply to mean "before," and "e'er" to be spelled and understood as "ere," which is the form here in F.

174. *nice* precise.

MALCOLM

What's the newest grief?

ROSS

175 That of an hour's age doth hiss the speaker;
Each minute teems a new one.

MACDUFF

How does my wife?

ROSS

Why, well.

MACDUFF

And all my children?

ROSS

Well too.

MACDUFF

The tyrant has not battered at their peace?

ROSS

No, they were well at peace when I did leave 'em.

MACDUFF

180 Be not a niggard of your speech: how goes't?

ROSS

When I came hither to transport the tidings
Which I have heavily borne, there ran a rumour
Of many worthy fellows that were out;
Which was to my belief witnessed the rather

---

175. *hiss the speaker*   cause the speaker to be hissed (since news an hour old is stale).

176. *teems*   gives birth to, produces.

177. The line is short, suggesting a pause marking Ross's confusion after the word "children."

183. *out*   i.e., armed and in the field.

185   For that I saw the tyrant's power afoot.
Now is the time of help; your eye in Scotland
Would create soldiers, make our women fight,
To doff their dire distress.

MALCOLM

Be't their comfort
We are coming thither. Gracious England hath
190   Lent us good Siward and ten thousand men;
An older and a better soldier none
That Christendom gives out.

ROSS

Would I could answer
This comfort with the like! But I have words
That would be howled out in the desert air,
Where hearing should not latch them.

MACDUFF

195   What concern they?
The general cause? or is it a fee-grief
Due to some single breast?

ROSS

No mind that's honest
But in it shares some woe, though the main part
Pertains to you alone.

---

185. *For that* because. *power* army.
189. *Gracious England* See line 43 and note.
191. *older* more experienced.
192. *gives out* reports.
195. *latch* catch.
196. *fee-grief* a personal sorrow: a man who holds property "in fee" has absolute ownership of it.
197. *honest* well-disposed, virtuous.

MACDUFF

If it be mine,
200 Keep it not from me; quickly let me have it.

ROSS

Let not your ears despise my tongue for ever,
Which shall possess them with the heaviest sound
That ever yet they heard.

MACDUFF

Humh! I guess at it.

ROSS

Your castle is surprised; your wife and babes
205 Savagely slaughtered. To relate the manner
Were, on the quarry of these murdered deer,
To add the death of you.

MALCOLM

Merciful Heaven!
[*To* MACDUFF] What, man, ne'er pull your hat upon your brows!
Give sorrow words; the grief that does not speak
210 Whispers the o'er-fraught heart and bids it break.

MACDUFF

My children too?

---

202. *heaviest* most grievous.

206. *quarry* the heap made of the deer killed in a hunt, and hence a pile of dead bodies. *deer* punning on "dear."

209–10. *grief . . . break* varying a favorite tag of Jacobean dramatists, from Seneca's play *Hippolytus*, line 607: *Curae leves loquuntur, ingentes stupent* ("Small cares speak out, great sorrows are struck dumb"); this tag was cited or translated in plays by Cyril Tourneur, John Webster, and John Ford, and in John Florio's English version of Montaigne's *Essays*.

210. *Whispers* i.e., whispers to. The verb was commonly used transitively, as here.

ROSS

Wife, children, servants, all

That could be found.

MACDUFF

And I must be from thence!

My wife killed too?

ROSS

I have said.

MALCOLM

Be comforted.

Let's make us med'cines of our great revenge,
215   To cure this deadly grief.

MACDUFF

He has no children.—All my pretty ones?
Did you say all? O Hell-kite! All?
What, all my pretty chickens and their dam
At one fell swoop?

MALCOLM

Dispute it like a man.

---

216. *He . . . children*   A.C. Bradley in his *Shakespearean Tragedy*,
pp. 489—92, strongly supported the view that this refers to Malcolm,
who can talk easily of comfort being childless; it is more often taken
as a reference to Macbeth, either in the sense that Macduff cannot
properly revenge himself, since Macbeth has no children, or in the
sense that if Macbeth had children of his own, he would not have sanc-
tioned the slaughter of Macduff's family. I think Macduff has Macbeth
in mind—despite Lady Macbeth's cry, "I have given suck" (see
I.vii.54—9 and note)—for there is no hint in the play that she and
Macbeth have a child living at this time.

220. *Dispute it*   strive against your affliction.

MACDUFF

220   I shall do so;
But I must also feel it as a man.
I cannot but remember such things were
That were most precious to me. Did Heaven look on,
And would not take their part? Sinful Macduff,
225   They were all struck for thee! Naught that I am,
Not for their own demerits, but for mine,
Fell slaughter on their souls. Heaven rest them now!

MALCOLM

Be this the whetstone of your sword, let grief
Convert to anger: blunt not the heart, enrage it.

MACDUFF

230   O I could play the woman with mine eyes,
And braggart with my tongue! But, gentle heavens,
Cut short all intermission. Front to front
Bring thou this fiend of Scotland and myself;
Within my sword's length set him; if he 'scape,
Heaven forgive him too!

MALCOLM

235   This tune goes manly.
Come, go we to the King; our power is ready;
Our lack is nothing but our leave. Macbeth
Is ripe for shaking, and the Powers above

---

225. *Naught*   wicked. Macduff sees their deaths as a divine punishment inflicted on him for his own sins.

235. *tune*   F has "time," probably the compositor's misreading of the manuscript.

236. *power*   army, as at line 185.

237. *Our . . . leave*   i.e., we have nothing more to do but take leave of King Edward.

238. *Powers*   See II.i.7 and note.

Put on their instruments. Receive what cheer you may;
240   The night is long that never finds the day.

Exeunt.

Act V, scene i: Enter a Doctor of Physic *and a* Waiting
Gentlewoman.

DOCTOR

I have two nights watched with you, but can perceive no truth
in your report. When was it she last walked?

GENTLEWOMAN

Since his majesty went into the field, I have seen her rise from
her bed, throw her night-gown upon her, unlock her closet, take
5   forth paper, fold it, write upon't, read it, afterwards seal it,
and again return to bed; yet all this while in a most fast sleep.

---

239. *Put . . . instruments*   arm themselves.

   scene i   The setting is Dunsinane Castle (see V.ii.12, V.iii.2), Macbeth's last stronghold; the action carries over from IV.iii, with no hint of an interval of time: Macbeth had a "power afoot" at IV.iii.185, and here is in "the field" (line 3). The armies opposing him have not yet reached Dunsinane, and are shown doing so in V.ii and V.iv. Lady Macbeth's words in this scene echo and sometimes amplify the dialogue relating to the murder of Duncan in II.i and II.ii. The scene is not in Holinshed, and Lady Macbeth is not mentioned in his account of the downfall and death of Macbeth; Shakespeare developed the character out of the bare sketch of Donwald's wife given in Holinshed's account of the murder of King Duff (see Appendix B, p. 171).

   3. *into the field*   i.e., out with his troops. *night-gown*   dressing gown (as at II.ii.70).

   4. *closet*   cabinet, or the place in which she keeps her valuables.

   5. *fold it . . . seal it*   Some critics have suggested that she is writing a letter to Macbeth, as though she would still seek to guide him; or she may simply be unburdening herself of that guilty secret which weighs upon her conscience.

DOCTOR

A great perturbation in nature, to receive at once the benefit
of sleep and do the effects of watching! In this slumb'ry agitation, besides her walking and other actual performances, what,
10 at any time, have you heard her say?

GENTLEWOMAN

That, sir, which I will not report after her.

DOCTOR

You may to me, and 'tis most meet you should.

GENTLEWOMAN

Neither to you nor anyone, having no witness to confirm my
speech.

   Enter LADY [MACBETH], *with a taper.*

15 Lo you, here she comes! This is her very guise, and, upon my
life, fast asleep. Observe her; stand close.

DOCTOR

How came she by that light?

GENTLEWOMAN

Why, it stood by her; she has light by her continually, 'tis her
command.

DOCTOR

20 You see her eyes are open.

---

7. *perturbation in nature* disorder in the human constitution: "nature" here means "the inherent power or force by which the physical
and mental activities of man are sustained" (OED).
 8. *do . . . watching* i.e., perform actions of wakefulness.
 8–9. *agitation* activity.
 9. *actual performances* actions carried out.
 15. *very guise* usual behavior.
 16. *stand close* stand aside, keep hidden.

GENTLEWOMAN

Ay, but their sense are shut.

DOCTOR

What is it she does now? Look how she rubs her hands.

GENTLEWOMAN

It is an accustomed action with her, to seem thus washing her hands. I have known her continue in this a quarter of an hour.

LADY MACBETH

25   Yet here's a spot.

DOCTOR

Hark! she speaks. I will set down what comes from her, to satisfy my remembrance the more strongly.

LADY MACBETH

Out, damned spot! out, I say!—One; two. Why, then, 'tis time to do't.—Hell is murky.—Fie, my lord, fie! a soldier, and
30   afeard? What need we fear who knows it, when none can call our power to accompt?—Yet who would have thought the old man to have had so much blood in him?

DOCTOR

Do you mark that?

---

21. *are*   after F, but often emended to "is." Shakespeare probably used "are," since the sense is of two eyes, referring back to line 20.

23–4. *seem . . . hands*   ironically recalling "A little water clears us of this deed" (II.ii.67).

27. *satisfy . . . remembrance*   i.e., help me remember.

28. *One; two*   She may be imagining a clock striking, but note that she gave Macbeth the signal to go to Duncan by striking on a bell (see II.i.32, 62).

30–31. *none . . . accompt*   i.e., our power is so great that no one can make us answer for what we do; "accompt" is an old form of "account."

LADY MACBETH

The Thane of Fife had a wife; where is she now?—What,
35   will these hands ne'er be clean?—No more o' that, my lord,
no more o' that! You mar all with this starting.

DOCTOR

Go to, go to; you have known what you should not.

GENTLEWOMAN

She has spoke what she should not, I am sure of that. Heaven
knows what she has known.

LADY MACBETH

40   Here's the smell of the blood still: all the perfumes of Arabia
will not sweeten this little hand. O, O, O!

DOCTOR

What a sigh is there! The heart is sorely charged.

GENTLEWOMAN

I would not have such a heart in my bosom for the dignity of
the whole body.

DOCTOR

45   Well, well, well.

GENTLEWOMAN

Pray God it be, sir.

DOCTOR

This disease is beyond my practice. Yet I have known those
which have walked in their sleep who have died holily in their
beds.

---

36. *You . . . starting*   See II.ii.58—63 and III.iv.62.
37. *Go to, go to*   expressing disapproval, as "come, come."
42. *sorely charged*   grievously burdened (with guilt).
43. *dignity*   worth.
47. *practice*   medical skill.

LADY MACBETH

50 Wash your hands, put on your night-gown, look not so pale:
I tell you yet again, Banquo's buried; he cannot come out on's
grave.

DOCTOR

Even so?

LADY MACBETH

To bed, to bed; there's knocking at the gate. Come, come, come,
55 come, give me your hand. What's done cannot be undone. To
bed, to bed, to bed!

Exit.

DOCTOR

Will she go now to bed?

GENTLEWOMAN

Directly.

DOCTOR

Foul whisp'rings are abroad. Unnatural deeds
60 Do breed unnatural troubles. Infected minds
To their deaf pillows will discharge their secrets.
More needs she the divine than the physician.
God, God forgive us all! Look after her,
Remove from her the means of all annoyance,
65 And still keep eyes upon her. So, good night.
My mind she has mated, and amazed my sight.
I think, but dare not speak.

---

51. *on's* i.e., of his.

55. *What's . . . undone* echoing her comment at III.ii.12.

59. *whisp'rings* rumors.

64. *annoyance* injury (to herself); he fears she may commit suicide, as she apparently does later; see V.viii.35–7.

66. *mated* baffled, bewildered.

GENTLEWOMAN

Good night, good doctor.

Exeunt.

Scene ii: Drum and colours. Enter MENTEITH, CAITHNESS, ANGUS, LENNOX, *Soldiers.*

MENTEITH

The English power is near, led on by Malcolm,
His uncle Siward, and the good Macduff.
Revenges burn in them; for their dear causes
Would to the bleeding and the grim alarm
Excite the mortified man.

ANGUS

5   Near Birnam Wood
Shall we well meet them; that way are they coming.

Scene ii We were told at IV.iii.182–3 of "worthy fellows" rising in Scotland against Macbeth; the rebel army is now seen, near Macbeth's stronghold of Dunsinane. Although no indication of time is given in these final scenes, the action moves swiftly—one scene flowing into the next—with a gathering pace to Macbeth's downfall. Many details, and much of the action, are taken directly from Holinshed's account (see Appendix B, p. 169).

2. *uncle* Holinshed, however, says that Duncan's wife was the daughter of Siward, making Siward Malcolm's grandfather (see Appendix B, p. 164). Perhaps this would have made Siward too old in relation to Malcolm and Duncan (whom Lady Macbeth calls "the old man" at V.i.31–2) for Shakespeare's conception.

3. *dear causes* deeply felt grounds for action; or "grievous wrongs" (Dover Wilson), if "dear" here has the meaning "severe," as at *Timon* V.i.226, "our dear peril."

4. *alarm* call to arms, or to battle.

5. *Excite . . . man* stir up an unconscious (or a dead) man; "mortified" means "insensible," whether from numbness or death.

6. *well* readily, easily.

CAITHNESS

Who knows if Donalbain be with his brother?

LENNOX

For certain, sir, he is not. I have a file
Of all the gentry: there is Siward's son,
10 And many unrough youths that even now
Protest their first of manhood.

MENTEITH

What does the tyrant?

CAITHNESS

Great Dunsinane he strongly fortifies.
Some say he's mad; others that lesser hate him
Do call it valiant fury; but, for certain,
15 He cannot buckle his distempered cause
Within the belt of rule.

ANGUS

Now does he feel
His secret murders sticking on his hands;
Now minutely revolts upbraid his faith-breach.
Those he commands move only in command,
20 Nothing in love. Now does he feel his title
Hang loose about him, like a giant's robe
Upon a dwarfish thief.

---

8. *file*   list.

10. *unrough*   i.e., smooth-faced, beardless (spelled "unruffe" in F).

11. *protest*   proclaim.

15. *distempered cause*   disordered affairs, or unruly party. Both
meanings are possible, and "distempered" also suggests sickness, looking forward to line 27 and the imagery of the next scene.

17. *sticking . . . hands*   recalling II.ii.60–3 and V.i.40–41.

18. *minutely*   (adj.) occurring every minute, very frequent. *faith-
breach*   treachery.

20. *Nothing*   (adv.) not at all.

MENTEITH

Who then shall blame
His pestered senses to recoil and start,
When all that is within him does condemn
Itself for being there?

CAITHNESS

25   Well, march we on,
To give obedience where 'tis truly owed.
Meet we the med'cine of the sickly weal,
And with him pour we in our country's purge
Each drop of us.

LENNOX

Or so much as it needs
30   To dew the sovereign flower and drown the weeds.
Make we our march towards Birnam.

Exeunt marching.

Scene iii: Enter MACBETH, Doctor, *and attendants.*

MACBETH

Bring me no more reports, let them fly all!
Till Birnam Wood remove to Dunsinane

---

23. *pestered* troubled. *to . . . start* i.e., for recoiling and shrinking (in fear or disgust). This kind of construction was not uncommon (see Abbott, 356).

27. *med'cine* the saving doctor, Malcolm; and see V.iii.50–54. *weal* state, or commonweal.

28–9. *And . . . us* as if their blood would itself be a medicine to cleanse the land.

30. *sovereign* royal (as referring to Malcolm), and healing (as a sovereign remedy).

Scene iii Macbeth is no longer in "the field" (V.i.3), but has retired to his castle on Dunsinane Hill.

1. *them* his thanes; see line 7.

I cannot taint with fear. What's the boy Malcolm?
Was he not born of woman? The spirits that know
5   All mortal consequences have pronounced me thus:
"Fear not, Macbeth; no man that's born of woman
Shall e'er have power upon thee." Then fly, false thanes,
And mingle with the English epicures!
The mind I sway by and the heart I bear
10   Shall never sag with doubt nor shake with fear.

Enter Servant.

The Devil damn thee black, thou cream-faced loon!
Where got'st thou that goose look?

SERVANT

There is ten thousand—

MACBETH

Geese, villain?

SERVANT

Soldiers, sir.

MACBETH

Go prick thy face, and over-red thy fear,

---

3. *taint*   weaken, become tainted.

4–7. *The . . . thee*   See IV.i.79–80.

5. *mortal consequences*   future events in human existence. The line is an alexandrine, and "consequences" is often emended to "consequence" to shorten it. *pronounced*   proclaimed.

8. *epicures*   gluttons; perhaps suggested by Holinshed's comment that "fine fare or riotous surfeit . . . came into the realm of Scotland with the *Englishmen*."

9. *sway*   control (myself).

11. *cream-faced*   white-faced (with fear). *loon*   rogue, worthless fellow.

12. *goose*   The goose was proverbially foolish or stupid, but Shakespeare also thought of geese as cowardly (see *Coriolanus* I.iv.34–6).

15   Thou lily-livered boy. What soldiers, patch?
     Death of thy soul! Those linen cheeks of thine
     Are counsellors to fear. What soldiers, wheyface?

SERVANT

The English force, so please you.

MACBETH

Take thy face hence.

                                       [*Exit* Servant.]
                    Seyton!—I am sick at heart

20   When I behold—Seyton, I say!—This push
     Will cheer me ever or disseat me now.
     I have lived long enough: my way of life
     Is fallen into the sere, the yellow leaf;
     And that which should accompany old age,

25   As honour, love, obedience, troops of friends,
     I must not look to have; but, in their stead,
     Curses, not loud but deep, mouth-honour, breath
     Which the poor heart would fain deny, and dare not.—
     Seyton!

Enter SEYTON.

---

15. *lily-livered*   cowardly. The liver was regarded as the seat of the passions generally, and of courage in particular. *patch*   fool; probably an Anglicization of the Italian word *pazzo*.

16. *of*   i.e., on.

17. *Are . . . fear*   i.e., make others afraid.

19. *Seyton*   pronounced "Seeton"; Shakespeare probably borrowed the name of Macbeth's last companion from the list of "new surnames" Holinshed says were taken up on the accession of Malcolm to the throne (see Appendix B, p. 170).

20. *push*   crisis, or attack.

21. *cheer*   punning on "chair" meaning "enthrone." *disseat*   unseat; "dis-eate" in F.

27. *mouth-honour*   Kenneth Muir notes a probable reference here to Isaiah 29:13, "this people when they be in trouble do honour me with their mouth and with their lips, but their heart is far from me."

SEYTON

What's your gracious pleasure?

MACBETH

30   What news more?

SEYTON

All is confirmed, my lord, which was reported.

MACBETH

I'll fight till from my bones my flesh be hacked.
Give me my armour.

SEYTON

'Tis not needed yet.

MACBETH

I'll put it on.
35 Send out moe horses, skirr the country round;
Hang those that talk of fear. Give me mine armour.—
How does your patient, doctor?

DOCTOR

Not so sick, my lord,
As she is troubled with thick-coming fancies
That keep her from her rest.

MACBETH

Cure her of that!
40 Canst thou not minister to a mind diseased,
Pluck from the memory a rooted sorrow,

---

35. *moe* more. *skirr* scour.
37. *How . . . doctor?* The doctor has been on-stage throughout the
scene, but only now do Macbeth's thoughts turn briefly to his wife.
39. *Cure her of* F2; "Cure of" (F) makes no sense, and emendation
is necessary. Wright suggested "Make cure of," which fits well since
Macbeth seems to be thinking more of himself than his wife in what
follows (see line 46).

Raze out the written troubles of the brain,
And with some sweet oblivious antidote
Cleanse the stuffed bosom of that perilous stuff
Which weighs upon the heart?

DOCTOR

45   Therein the patient
Must minister to himself.

MACBETH

Throw physic to the dogs; I'll none of it.—
[*To* SEYTON] Come, put mine armour on. Give me my staff.
Seyton, send out.—Doctor, the thanes fly from me.—
50   [*To* SEYTON] Come, sir, despatch.—If thou couldst, doctor, cast
The water of my land, find her disease,
And purge it to a sound and pristine health,
I would applaud thee to the very echo,
That should applaud again. [*To Seyton*] Pull't off, I say.—
55   What rhubarb, senna, or what purgative drug
Would scour these English hence? Hear'st thou of them?

---

42. *Raze out*   erase.

43. *oblivious*   producing forgetfulness.

44. *stuffed . . . stuff*   Many editors have proposed emending one of these words, for the repetition is awkward and lacks point, but none of the suggestions put forward seem convincing; "stained" and "fraught" (instead of "stuffed") are perhaps the best.

48. *staff*   i.e., general's baton.

50. *despatch*   hurry up.

50–51. *Cast . . . disease*   It was common practice to diagnose diseases by inspecting the urine, or "casting water."

55. *senna*   emended in F4 from "Cyme" (F), which could be a compositor's misreading of "cynna," a conceivable spelling of "senna." However the F spelling arose, "senna" is most appropriate here as a well-known purge. The word "cyme," a botanical term meaning a kind of flower head on a plant, is not recorded earlier than 1725 in *OED*.

DOCTOR

Ay, my good lord. Your royal preparation
Makes us hear something.

MACBETH

[*To Seyton*]   Bring it after me.—
I will not be afraid of death and bane
60   Till Birnam Forest come to Dunsinane.
                              [*Exeunt* MACBETH *and* SEYTON.]

DOCTOR

Were I from Dunsinane away and clear,
Profit again should hardly draw me here.

                                                            Exit.

Scene iv: Drum and colours. Enter MALCOLM, SIWARD, MACDUFF,
Siward's Son, MENTEITH, CAITHNESS, ANGUS, [LENNOX, ROSS,] *and
soldiers marching.*

MALCOLM

Cousins, I hope the days are near at hand
That chambers will be safe.

MENTEITH

                    We doubt it nothing.

---

59. *bane*   ruin, destruction.
Scene iv   The union of Scottish rebels and English invaders promised in V.ii has taken place, and the combined forces have reached the
edge of Birnam Wood. Lennox (present in V.ii) and Ross (who clearly
fights in Malcolm's army, see V.viii) are not named in the entrance
in F, but both should appear here.
1. *Cousins*   the term used by a sovereign addressing his nobles.
2. *chambers . . . safe*   i.e., we can sleep in safety; see III.vi.34—5.
nothing   (adv.) not at all.

SIWARD

What wood is this before us?

MENTEITH

The Wood of Birnam.

MALCOLM

Let every soldier hew him down a bough

5   And bear't before him; thereby shall we shadow

The numbers of our host, and make discovery

Err in report of us.

SOLDIER

It shall be done.

SIWARD

We learn no other but the confident tyrant

Keeps still in Dunsinane, and will endure

Our setting down before't.

MALCOLM

10   'Tis his main hope;

For where there is advantage to be gone,

Both more and less have given him the revolt,

And none serve with him but constrained things

Whose hearts are absent too.

---

4. See Holinshed (Appendix B, p. 169).

5. *shadow*   screen, conceal.

6. *discovery*   reconnaissance; see *Lear* V.i.53.

10. *setting down*   making camp (for a siege).

11. *where . . . gone*   i.e., where there is a chance to escape; "gone" is generally adopted as an emendation of "given" (F), which may have been an anticipation by the compositor of "given" in line 12. The repetition lacks point (see V.iii.44 also) and makes poor sense in line 11, though the interpretation "when given the opportunity" can be forced upon it.

12. *more and less*   high and low. *given . . . revolt*   rebelled against him.

MACDUFF

                 Let our just censures

15   Attend the true event, and put we on
Industrious soldiership.

SIWARD

              The time approaches
That will with due decision make us know
What we shall say we have and what we owe.
Thoughts speculative their unsure hopes relate,

20   But certain issue strokes must arbitrate,
Towards which, advance the war.

                            Exeunt marching.

Scene v: Enter MACBETH, SEYTON, *and soldiers, with drum and colours.*

MACBETH

Hang out our banners on the outward walls.
The cry is still, "They come!" Our castle's strength

14–15. *Let . . . event*   let our just estimate wait on the actual outcome; i.e., we shall be able to judge the situation properly when we see the result of the battle.

18. *What . . . owe*   what we shall be able to say we have (i.e., after the battle) and what remains to be done, or is owed to duty.

19–20. *Thoughts . . . arbitrate*   i.e., speculation tends to reflect wishful thinking, or hopes that are not sure; the issue must be decided in battle.

Scene v   At Dunsinane again, where the siege is in progress. Macbeth enters with his "army," suggested—as was Malcolm's—by a handful of actors with martial trappings, here a drum and banners.

1. *outward walls*   outer walls; the outer wall, or bailey, of a medieval castle enclosed a courtyard and an inner wall, with the keep, or central stronghold, behind the inner wall.

Will laugh a siege to scorn; here let them lie
Till famine and the ague eat them up.
5 Were they not forced with those that should be ours,
We might have met them dareful, beard to beard,
And beat them backward home.

                      A cry within of women.
                      What is that noise?

SEYTON

It is the cry of women, my good lord.

                      [*Exit* SEYTON.]

MACBETH

I have almost forgot the taste of fears.
10 The time has been, my senses would have cooled
To hear a night-shriek, and my fell of hair
Would at a dismal treatise rouse and stir
As life were in't. I have supped full with horrors;
Direness, familiar to my slaughterous thoughts,
Cannot once start me.

                [*Enter* SEYTON.]
15   Wherefore was that cry?

SEYTON

The Queen, my lord, is dead.

MACBETH

She should have died hereafter;

---

5. *forced* reinforced.
6. *dareful* defiantly.
10. *my . . . cooled* i.e., I would have become cold with fear.
11. *fell of hair* skin covered in hair, i.e., all his hair.
12. *treatise* story.
15. *start me* make me start.
17. *hereafter* i.e., at some other period, when her death would have had meaning for me. In his present difficulties Macbeth cannot react to this news.

144

There would have been a time for such a word.—
Tomorrow, and tomorrow, and tomorrow,
20   Creeps in this petty pace from day to day,
To the last syllable of recorded time;
And all our yesterdays have lighted fools
The way to dusty death. Out, out, brief candle!
Life's but a walking shadow, a poor player
25   That struts and frets his hour upon the stage
And then is heard no more. It is a tale
Told by an idiot, full of sound and fury,
Signifying nothing.

Enter a Messenger.

Thou com'st to use thy tongue; thy story quickly.

MESSENGER

30   Gracious my lord,
I should report that which I say I saw,
But know not how to do't.

MACBETH

Well, say, sir.

---

18. *word*   announcement (of her death).

22—4. *lighted . . . shadow*   These lines echo various Biblical images related to the central idea of life as a light or candle; see especially Psalms 22:15, "the dust of death"; Job 18:6, "The light shall be dark in his dwelling, and his candle shall be put out with him"; Job 14:1—2, "Man . . . fleeth as it were a shadow, and never continueth in one state"; Psalms 39:7, "For man walketh in a vain shadow" (*Book of Common Prayer*). The Biblical background helps to give these lines their density and evocative power.

24. *poor*   As Kittredge notes, the word expresses pity; it does not primarily suggest a bad actor, though this idea is perhaps present.

26—7. *It . . . Told*   See Psalms 90:9, "we bring our years to an end, as it were a tale that is told."

MESSENGER

As I did stand my watch upon the hill,
I looked toward Birnam, and anon methought
The Wood began to move.

MACBETH

35   Liar and slave!

MESSENGER

Let me endure your wrath if't be not so:
Within this three mile may you see it coming;
I say, a moving grove.

MACBETH

If thou speak'st false,
Upon the next tree shall thou hang alive
40 Till famine cling thee. If thy speech be sooth,
I care not if thou dost for me as much.—
I pall in resolution and begin
To doubt th' equivocation of the fiend
That lies like truth. "Fear not, till Birnam Wood
45 Do come to Dunsinane," and now a wood
Comes toward Dunsinane.—Arm, arm, and out!—
If this which he avouches does appear,
There is nor flying hence nor tarrying here.
I gin to be aweary of the sun,

---

33. *stand my watch*   take my turn of duty as lookout.
37. *mile*   a common plural form, still in spoken use.
40. *cling*   shrivel. *sooth*   true.
42. *pall*   fail, as at *Hamlet* V.ii.9, "When our deep plots do pall."
This is Dr. Johnson's suggested correction of "pull" (F); the compositor might easily have read *u* for *a*, or might have been faced with a
spelling like that in the *Hamlet* passage ("paule") and taken his choice.
"Pull in" could only mean "rein in" (like a horse), and the idea of
Macbeth actively undermining his own confidence jars here.
49. *gin*   begin.

50 And wish th' estate o' th' world were now undone.—
Ring the alarum bell!—Blow, wind! come, wrack!
At least we'll die with harness on our back.

Exeunt.

Scene vi: Drum and colours. Enter MALCOLM, SIWARD, MACDUFF,
and their army, with boughs.

MALCOLM

Now near enough; your leavy screens throw down,
And show like those you are. [*To* SIWARD] You, worthy uncle,
Shall with my cousin, your right noble son,
Lead our first battle. Worthy Macduff and we
5 Shall take upon's what else remains to do,
According to our order.

SIWARD

Fare you well.
Do we but find the tyrant's power tonight,
Let us be beaten if we cannot fight.

---

50. *th' estate . . . world* the condition, or order, of the universe.
51. *alarum bell* the bell that summons the men to the final battle.
It is also a kind of knell for Macbeth, recalling the bell that rang for
Duncan (see II.i.62–3). *wrack* ruin.
52. *harness* armor.
Scene vi The army includes the other Scottish lords present in V.iv,
but the casual stage direction does not name them.
2. *uncle* See V.ii.2 and note.
4. *first battle* first army or line of attack (we now say "battalion,"
which has absorbed this meaning of "battle").
7. *power* army.

MACDUFF

Make all our trumpets speak; give them all breath,
10   Those clamorous harbingers of blood and death.

                              Exeunt. Alarums continued.

Scene vii: Enter MACBETH.

MACBETH

They have tied me to a stake; I cannot fly,
But bearlike I must fight the course. What's he
That was not born of woman? Such a one
Am I to fear, or none.

---

10. *harbingers*   forerunners; see I.iv.45 and note.

S.D. *Alarums*   i.e., calls to arms. There is no break between this scene and the next. The "trumpets" of line 9 go on sounding and skirmishes begin, which were no doubt represented on Shakespeare's stage roughly as they would commonly be done today, with a few pairs of actors dueling or small groups driving one another across the stage. A good deal of noise, movement, and a hint of smoke can create a turbulence out of which the emergence of a central figure (Macbeth, for instance, in the next scene) is strikingly effective.

Scene vii   The battle continues to rage throughout this scene; the stage doors at the Globe may have been used to focus the fighting and suggest entry into or out of the courtyard of Dunsinane Castle. The action is fluid, and new "scenes" within the scene occur at lines 13, 23, and 30 (where, in fact, most editors begin scene viii). Macbeth's final stand is Shakespeare's invention; according to Holinshed, Macbeth fled when he saw the numbers of Malcolm's army, and was pursued and killed by Malcolm (see Appendix B, p. 169).

2. *bearlike . . . course*   A popular sport of Shakespeare's time was bear baiting, in which a bear was chained to a stake in an arena and several large dogs were set upon him. Macbeth is trapped within the "arena," or the walls, of his castle and cannot fly; but like the bear's, his last fight can be ferocious. "Course" was a common term for "bout."

Enter YOUNG SIWARD.

YOUNG SIWARD

What is thy name?

MACBETH

5   Thou'lt be afraid to hear it.

YOUNG SIWARD

No; though thou call'st thyself a hotter name
Than any is in Hell.

MACBETH

       My name's Macbeth.

YOUNG SIWARD

The Devil himself could not pronounce a title
More hateful to mine ear.

MACBETH

         No, nor more fearful.

YOUNG SIWARD

10   Thou liest, abhorrèd tyrant! With my sword
I'll prove the lie thou speak'st.

          Fight, and YOUNG SIWARD *slain.*

MACBETH

               Thou wast born of woman;
But swords I smile at, weapons laugh to scorn,
Brandished by man that's of a woman born.

           Exit.

---

4. S.D. YOUNG SIWARD Macbeth's one fight before he meets Macduff is with a boy (see V.viii.6); the encounter indicates Macbeth's prowess, but brings him little credit.

13. *man . . . born* The power of this phrase derives partly from its Biblical usage as a way of referring to all mankind; see, for instance, Matthew 11:11.

Alarums. Enter MACDUFF.

MACDUFF

That way the noise is. Tyrant, show thy face!
25 If thou be'st slain and with no stroke of mine,
My wife and children's ghosts will haunt me still.
I cannot strike at wretched kerns, whose arms
Are hired to bear their staves; either thou, Macbeth,
Or else my sword with an unbattered edge
20 I sheathe again undeeded. There thou shouldst be.
By this great clatter, one of greatest note
Seems bruited. Let me find him, Fortune!
And more I beg not.

Exit. Alarums.

Enter MALCOLM *and* [OLD] SIWARD.

OLD SIWARD

This way, my lord. The castle's gently rendered;
25 The tyrant's people on both sides do fight;
The noble thanes do bravely in the war;
The day almost itself professes yours,
And little is to do.

---

13. S.D. *Alarums . . .* MACDUFF Presumably in the disturbance following Macbeth's exit, Young Siward's body is carried off-stage. The body is not seen by Macduff, or by Old Siward, who enters at line 23, and in V.viii.10 the body is reported as "brought off the field."

17. *kerns* mercenaries (properly, Irish foot soldiers; see I.ii.13 and note).

18. *staves* spears (literally, the shafts of their weapons).

22. *bruited* announced (from the French *bruit*, meaning "noise"). The line is a syllable short, perhaps allowing for a pause after this word.

23. S.D. SIWARD See S.D. following line 13, and note above.

24. *rendered* surrendered.

MALCOLM

We have met with foes
That strike beside us.

OLD SIWARD

Enter, sir, the castle.

Exeunt. Alarum.

Enter MACBETH.

MACBETH

30   Why should I play the Roman fool and die
On my own sword? Whiles I see lives, the gashes
Do better upon them.

Enter MACDUFF.

MACDUFF

Turn, Hell-hound, turn!

MACBETH

Of all men else I have avoided thee.
But get thee back, my soul is too much charged
With blood of thine already.

MACDUFF

35   I have no words;
My voice is in my sword, thou bloodier villain
Than terms can give thee out!

Fight. Alarum.

---

29. *strike beside us*   This could mean "deliberately miss us," "strike wide of us," or "fight on our side."

29. S.D. *Enter* MACBETH   Most editors since Pope have begun a new scene here, although there is no scene division in F.

30. *Roman fool*   In Shakespeare's Roman plays, suicide is the usual way out for defeated generals like Brutus and Antony.

31. *lives*   i.e., enemies alive.

MACBETH

               Thou losest labour.
As easy mayest thou the intrenchant air
With thy keen sword impress as make me bleed.
40   Let fall thy blade on vulnerable crests;
I bear a charmèd life, which must not yield
To one of woman born.

MACDUFF

          Despair thy charm,
And let the angel whom thou still hast served
Tell thee, Macduff was from his mother's womb
45   Untimely ripped.

MACBETH

Accursèd be that tongue that tells me so,
For it hath cowed my better part of man!
And be these juggling fiends no more believed,
That palter with us in a double sense,
50   That keep the word of promise to our ear
And break it to our hope. I'll not fight with thee.

MACDUFF

Then yield thee, coward,
And live to be the show and gaze o' th' time.

---

38. *intrenchant*   incapable of being cut.

39. *impress*   mark, imprint.

42. *Despair*   i.e., despair of; common usage until the eighteenth century.

43. *angel*   i.e., bad angel; compare IV.iii.22. *still*   always.

47. *better part*   i.e., his mind, or spirit (as in Sonnet LXXIV.8: "My spirit is thine, the better part of me").

48. *juggling*   deceiving.

49. *palter*   equivocate.

We'll have thee, as our rarer monsters are,
55 Painted upon a pole, and underwrit,
"Here may you see the tyrant."

MACBETH

                 I will not yield,
To kiss the ground before young Malcolm's feet,
And to be baited with the rabble's curse.
Though Birnam Wood be come to Dunsinane,
60 And thou opposed, being of no woman born,
Yet I will try the last. Before my body
I throw my warlike shield. Lay on, Macduff,
And damned be him that first cries, "Hold, enough!"
Exeunt fighting. Alarums. [Re-]enter fighting, and MACBETH
slain.

Scene viii: Retreat and flourish. Enter, with drum and colours,
MALCOLM, [OLD] SIWARD, ROSS, *Thanes, and soldiers.*

MALCOLM

I would the friends we miss were safe arrived.

54–6. *thee . . . tyrant* i.e., his painted effigy, mounted on a pole,
will advertise where he is kept in captivity, like a rare monster, for
public display. Such shows seem to have been popular in Shakespeare's
London (see *Tempest* II.ii.30–37).

61. *try the last* i.e., fight to the end.

63. S.D. *fighting . . . slain* Elizabethan actors were good swords-
men, and the fight between Macduff and Macbeth would have been ex-
citingly staged, with the tension and suspense sustained until the final
death blow.

Scene viii No scene is marked here in F, but Pope was right to in-
troduce a division; as the fighting and "alarums" die away, Malcolm
and his army enter in triumph by another door, and the scene appears
to have shifted from the "field" (line 10) of V.vii to the interior of
the surrendered castle.

1. *arrived* i.e., here in the castle, from the battlefield.

OLD SIWARD

Some must go off; and yet by these I see
So great a day as this is cheaply bought.

MALCOLM

Macduff is missing, and your noble son.

ROSS

5 Your son, my lord, has paid a soldier's debt.
He only lived but till he was a man,
The which no sooner had his prowess confirmed
In the unshrinking station where he fought
But like a man he died.

OLD SIWARD

Then he is dead?

ROSS

10 Ay, and brought off the field. Your cause of sorrow
Must not be measured by his worth, for then
It hath no end.

OLD SIWARD

Had he his hurts before?

ROSS

Ay, on the front.

OLD SIWARD

Why then, God's soldier be he!
Had I as many sons as I have hairs,
15 I would not wish them to a fairer death;
And so, his knell is knolled.

---

2. *go off*   as from the stage of life; i.e., die. *these*   his companions.
5–19. See Holinshed's account of Young Siward's death (Appendix
B, p. 170).
8. *unshrinking station*   post in which he stood firm.
14. *hairs*   a pun on "heirs."

MALCOLM

　　　　　　　　He's worth more sorrow,
And that I'll spend for him.

OLD SIWARD

　　　　　　　　He's worth no more;
They say he parted well, and paid his score,
And so, God be with him! Here comes newer comfort.

Enter MACDUFF, *with* MACBETH's *head.*

MACDUFF

20　Hail, King! for so thou art. Behold, where stands
Th' usurper's cursèd head: the time is free!
I see thee compassed with thy kingdom's pearl
That speak my salutation in their minds,
Whose voices I desire aloud with mine;
Hail, King of Scotland!

ALL

25　　　　　Hail, King of Scotland!

　　　　　　　　　　　　　　　Flourish.

---

18. *parted*　died.

20. *stands*　presumably mounted on a pole, as Holinshed reports that Macduff "set it upon a pole, and brought it unto Malcolm" (see Appendix B, p. 170).

21. *the time is free*　i.e., the world is free from the yoke of tyranny. For "time" meaning "society at large," "the age," etc., see I.v.61–2 and note.

22. *compassed . . . pearl*　i.e., encircled by your kingdom's choicest men (or nobility); the image suggests a crown of pearl.

MALCOLM

We shall not spend a large expense of time
Before we reckon with your several loves
And make us even with you. My thanes and kinsmen,
Henceforth be earls, the first that ever Scotland
30   In such an honour named. What's more to do,
Which would be planted newly with the time—
As calling home our exiled friends abroad
That fled the snares of watchful tyranny,
Producing forth the cruel ministers
35   Of this dead butcher and his fiend-like queen,
Who, as 'tis thought, by self and violent hands
Took off her life—this, and what needful else
That calls upon us, by the grace of Grace
We will perform in measure, time, and place.
40   So, thanks to all at once and to each one,
Whom we invite to see us crowned at Scone.

              Flourish. Exeunt omnes.

27–8. *Before . . . you*   i.e., before we reward you for your particular services and pay our debts to you.

28–9. *My . . . earls*   taken from Holinshed; the rank was above thane.

34. *Producing forth*   bringing to light.

36. *self*   i.e., her own; see V.i.64 and note.

38. *grace of Grace*   i.e., by the grace of God. This phrase recalls the play with the word "grace" in IV.iii; see especially IV.iii.23–4 and 159.

39. *measure*   due order.

41. *Scone*   See II.iv.31 and note.

APPENDIX A

A Shakespeare Chronology

Some Important Dates Relating to Shakespeare's Life, and to MACBETH in Particular

1557 (about). John Shakespeare of Stratford-on-Avon marries Mary Arden (they are to have four daughters, all but one of whom dies young, and four sons, including William).

1557 November 17. Accession of Queen Elizabeth.

1564 April 26. Christening of William Shakespeare, eldest son and third child of John and Mary.

1582 November 17. The license for Shakespeare's marriage to Anne Hathaway of Stratford is issued by the bishop's office in Worcester. The bishop's register (mistakenly?) calls his wife Anne Whately of Temple Grafton. The marriage may have been legally contracted earlier, though without a church ceremony.

1583 May 26. Shakespeare's first child, Susanna, is christened at Stratford.

1585 February 2. Christening of twins, Hamnet and Judith Shakespeare, at Stratford.

1585–91 There are no known references to this period of Shakespeare's life.

1592 First reference to a performance of a play by Shakespeare: *Henry VI, Part 1*.

1593 Shakespeare dedicates his first published work, the poem *Venus and Adonis*, to the Earl of Southampton. Christopher Marlowe, Shakespeare's leading rival as a dramatist, is killed in a tavern brawl.

1594 After a period of disorder caused by the plague and frequent bankruptcies among dramatic companies, two groups of players survive: the Lord Admiral's Men, run by Philip Henslowe and his actor son-in-law Edward Alleyn, and the Lord Chamberlain's

Men, run by Cuthbert Burbage and his actor son Richard. Shakespeare's company is the Lord Chamberlain's Men.

1596 August 11. Hamnet, Shakespeare's only son, buried in Stratford.

1597 Shakespeare buys New Place, a house in Stratford.

1599 The Globe Theatre opens, built and run by a syndicate of the Lord Chamberlain's Men, with Shakespeare as one of the shareholders.

1599–1600 Shakespeare turns from writing histories and comedies to tragedies and "dark" comedies; *Hamlet* (about 1600) is followed by *Othello, King Lear,* and *Macbeth*. The Lord Admiral's Men open the Fortune Theatre to rival the Globe.

1603 Death of Queen Elizabeth. King James I (already James VI of Scotland) succeeds her. The acting companies are taken under royal patronage; Shakespeare's company is now known as the King's Men, and the Lord Admiral's company as Prince Henry's Men.

1605 Gunpowder Plot, aimed at blowing up King and Parliament, is discovered; the main conspirators are killed or captured.

1606 March. Henry Garnet, Superior of the Jesuit order in England, is tried and executed for complicity in the Gunpowder Plot; Shakespeare alludes to the trial in *Macbeth* (II.iii).

1606–7 *Macbeth* echoed in Thomas Middleton's *The Puritan* and in *The Knight of the Burning Pestle,* by Francis Beaumont and John Fletcher.

1606–8 Shakespeare engaged in writing plays on classical themes, *Timon of Athens, Antony and Cleopatra,* and *Coriolanus*.

1608–9 Shakespeare's company acquires a roofed, indoor theater, the Blackfriars, for winter performances. He begins to write romances, first *Pericles,* then *Cymbeline, The Winter's Tale,* and *The Tempest*.

1609 February 2. Ben Jonson's *Masque of Queens,* featuring witches, is performed.

1610 (about). Thomas Middleton's *The Witch* written, with witches' songs that were later incorporated into *Macbeth*.

1613 June 29. The Globe Theatre burns down during a performance of *Henry VIII,* probably Shakespeare's last play.

1616 April 23. Shakespeare dies, and is buried in Stratford, where he had gone to live about 1610.

1623 The First Folio edition of Shakespeare's plays, gathered by his fellow actors John Heminges and Henry Condell, is published late in the year.

1673 The Quarto edition of *Macbeth* is published, containing text of the song "Come away" (III.v).

1674 Sir William D'Avenant's version of *Macbeth* is printed, containing text of the song "Black spirits" (IV.i).

APPENDIX B

Sources for MACBETH

The basic source for much of the action of the play is Raphael Holinshed's *Chronicles of England, Scotland and Ireland* (3 vols., 1587), a revised and enlarged edition of a work first published in 1577. There Shakespeare found, in the account of the murder of King Duff, a design for the murder of Duncan in *Macbeth*, and he also made use of the stories of Macbeth's encounter with the Weird Sisters, his dealings with Banquo, his persecution of Macduff and overthrow by Malcolm. Some scholars have argued that Shakespeare drew from other writings, notably William Stewart's *Book of the Chronicles of Scotland*, which was not printed until 1858 and George Buchanan's *Rerum Scoticarum Historia*, printed in 1582, but Shakespeare was certainly capable of inventing what little these add to Holinshed. He did know Samuel Harsnet's *Declaration of Egregious Popish Impostures* (1603), which he had used in writing *King Lear*, and probably Reginald Scot's *Discovery of Witchcraft* (1584); these very likely provided suggestions for the presentation of witchcraft in *Macbeth*.

Some important characters and scenes in *Macbeth* were invented by Shakespeare or expanded from mere hints in Holinshed. Shakespeare developed Lady Macbeth from a bare sketch, and he created the Porter and Lady Macduff. The banquet and the appearance of the Ghost of Banquo (III.iv), Macbeth's encounter with the Witches in Act IV, scene i, Lady Macbeth's sleepwalking scene (V.i) and her death in Act V, scene v, were all Shakespeare's invention. He departed from Holinshed's narrative in other respects, making Duncan, for instance, old and venerable (II.ii.12–13), although Holinshed describes him as a younger man and a weak king. Holinshed tells us that Macbeth ruled for seventeen years, and was an excellent king for much of that time, but Shakespeare telescopes the passage of time between the murder of Duncan and the murder of Banquo, and omits the years of good rule. According to Holinshed, Banquo was one of a group of conspirators who helped to kill Duncan, but Shakespeare turned this ancestor of King James into an attractive and virtuous figure. Holinshed reports that Macbeth himself besieged Macduff's castle with a great force, while Shakespeare has Macbeth send murderers there (IV.ii). Finally, Holinshed says that Macbeth fled from Dunsinane and was pursued by Macduff, whereas Shakespeare gives Macbeth a last heroic stand before his death at Dunsinane. These are the major innovations in Shakespeare's presentation, but other differences between *Chronicles* and play can be studied in the extracts from Holinshed printed below.

Other possible influences on Shakespeare in writing *Macbeth* include Seneca's play *Agamemnon*, as translated by Jasper Heywood (1581), and King James I's own writings, especially his *Demonology* (1597); see Introduction. The sources of *Macbeth*, both established and speculative, are discussed at length in Kenneth Muir's *Shakespeare's Sources* (London, 1957), I, 167—86, and by Muriel Bradbrook in *Shakespeare Survey*, 4 (Cambridge, 1951), pp. 35—48.

Holinshed's CHRONICLES (1587)

The following extracts are taken from the *Chronicles of Scotland* (Vol. II, pp. 150—76) and the *Chronicles of England* (Vol. I, pp. 192, 195). The punctuation and spelling have been modernized. References to *Macbeth* are given in square brackets within the extracts in those places where the wording of the play is close to Holinshed's.

The first passage relates chiefly to Act I, scene ii. By the historical method of succession, Macbeth *could* have succeeded Duncan, for the inheritance of the throne in Scotland at that time did not automatically go to the next of kin; rather, the successor was designated from among a group of kinsmen. By nominating his eldest son Malcolm as heir (I.iv.37—40), Duncan thwarted Macbeth's very good chance of becoming king. Shakespeare, however, makes no reference to the fact that Macbeth has had a genuine grievance against Duncan.

"After Malcolm succeeded his nephew Duncan, the son of his daughter Beatrice: for Malcolm had two daughters, the one which was this Beatrice, being given in marriage unto one Abbanath Crinen, a man of great nobility and Thane of the Isles and west parts of Scotland, bore of that marriage the foresaid Duncan; the other, called Doada, was married unto Sinell, the Thane of Glamis, by whom she had issue one Macbeth, a valiant gentleman [I.ii.24] and one that if he had not been somewhat cruel of nature might have been thought most worthy the government of a realm. On the other part, Duncan was so soft and gentle of nature [I.vii.16–17] that the people wished the inclinations and manners of these two cousins to have been so tempered and interchangeably bestowed betwixt them, that where the one had too much of clemency and the other of cruelty, the mean virtue betwixt these two extremities might have reigned by indifferent partition in them both; so should Duncan have proved a worthy king, and Macbeth an excellent captain.

"Banquo, the Thane of Lochaber, of whom the House of the Stewarts is descended, the which by order of lineage hath now for a long time enjoyed the crown of Scotland, even till these our days [IV.i.111–23], as he gathered the finances due to the King . . . being assailed by a number of rebels . . . had much ado to get away with life. . . . Yet escaping their hands . . . he repaired to the court, where, making his complaint to the King in most earnest wise, he purchased at length that the offenders were sent for by a sergeant-at-arms [I.ii.3]. . . ."

The rebels killed the King's messenger and feared that he would send an army against them.

"Macdowald, one of great estimation among them . . . took upon him to be chief captain of all such rebels as would stand against the King. . . . He used also such subtle persuasions and forged allurements that in a small time he had gotten together a mighty power of men; for out of the Western Isles there came unto him a great multitude of people, offering themselves to assist him in that rebellious quarrel, and out of Ireland in hope of the spoil came no small number of kerns and galloglasses [I.ii.9–13], offering gladly to serve under him, whither it should please him to lead them."

Macdowald defeated the army sent against him by Duncan, took prisoner its captain, Malcolm, and beheaded him. Duncan called a council of nobles to advise him.

"At length Macbeth, speaking much against the King's softness and overmuch slackness in punishing offenders, . . . promised notwithstanding, if the charge were committed unto him and Banquo, so to order the matter that the rebels should be shortly vanquished and quite put down, and that not so much as one of them should be found to make resistance within the country.

"And even so it came to pass: for being sent forth with a new power, at his entering into Lochaber, the fame of his coming put the enemies in such fear that a great number of them stole secretly away from their captain Macdowald, who, nevertheless enforced thereto, gave battle unto Macbeth, with the residue which remained with him; but being overcome and fleeing for refuge into a castle ... at length when he saw how he could neither defend the hold any longer against his enemies, nor yet upon surrender be suffered to depart with life saved, he first slew his wife and children and lastly himself, lest if he had yielded simply, he should have been executed in most cruel wise for an example to others."

Macbeth entered the castle, found Macdowald's body, and "remitting no piece of his cruel nature," had the head cut off and sent as a present to Duncan.

"Thus was justice and law restored again to the old accustomed course by the diligent means of Macbeth. Immediately whereupon word came that Sueno, King of Norway [I.ii.60–61], was arrived in Fife with a puissant army to subdue the whole realm of Scotland."

Holinshed relates the course of the wars against Sueno, how the Scots, led by Duncan, Macbeth, and Banquo, were at first defeated, then overcame the Danes by a trick, sending them food drugged with the juice of "mekilwoort berries," or deadly nightshade (a possible source for I.iii.84–5). Macbeth and his army carried out the final slaughter, from which Sueno escaped back to Denmark with one ship. While the Scots rejoiced, a new Danish fleet brought an army, sent by King Canute of England, to avenge the defeat of Sueno, his brother.

"To resist these enemies, which were already landed and busy in spoiling [i.e., despoiling] the country, Macbeth and Banquo were sent with the King's authority, who, having with them a convenient power, encountered the enemies, slew part of them and chased the other to their ships. They that escaped, and got once to their ships, obtained of Macbeth for a great sum of gold that such of their friends as were slain at this last bickering might be buried in Saint Colme's Inch [I.ii.61–4]."

So peace was made between the Scots and the Danes. There follow the stories of Macbeth's meeting with the Weird Sisters, and the death of Duncan, which relate to the action beginning in Act I, scene iii, and

ending in Act II, scene iii. The murder of Duncan in the play was
based on another story told by Holinshed, of the killing of King Duff
(see below, p. 166).

"Shortly after happened a strange and uncouth wonder, which
afterward was the cause of much trouble in the realm of Scotland, as
ye shall after hear. It fortuned as Macbeth and Banquo journeyed towards Forres, where the King then lay, they were sporting by the way
together without other company save only themselves, passing through
the woods and fields, when suddenly in the midst of a laund [i.e., a
glade], there met them three women in strange and wild apparel, resembling creatures of elder world [i.e., ancient times], whom when
they attentively beheld, wondering much at the sight; the first of
them spake and said, 'All hail Macbeth, Thane of Glamis' (for he had
lately entered into that dignity and office by the death of his father
Sinell). The second of them said, 'Hail Macbeth, Thane of Cawdor.'
But the third said, 'All hail Macbeth, that hereafter shalt be King of
Scotland' [I.iii.48—50].

"Then Banquo: 'What manner of women,' saith he, 'are you, that
seem so little favourable unto me, whereas to my fellow here, besides
high offices, ye assign also the kingdom, appointing forth nothing for
me at all' [I.iii.54—7]. 'Yes,' saith the first of them, 'we promise greater
benefits unto thee than unto him, for he shall reign indeed, but with
an unlucky end: neither shall he leave any issue behind him to succeed in his place, where contrarily thou indeed shall not reign at all, but
of thee those shall be born which shall govern the Scottish kingdom by
long order of continual descent' [I.iii.67]. Herewith the foresaid women
vanished immediately out of their sight [I.iii.78, stage direction]. This
was reputed at first but some vain fantastical illusion [I.iii.53] by
Macbeth and Banquo, in so much that Banquo would call Macbeth
in jest King of Scotland; and Macbeth again would call him, in sport
likewise, the father of many kings. But afterwards the common opinion
was that these women were either the Weird Sisters [I.iii.32], that is
(as ye would say) the goddesses of destiny, or else some nymphs or
fairies, indued with knowledge of prophecy by their necromantical
science, because everything came to pass as they had spoken. For
shortly after, the Thane of Cawdor being condemned at Forres of
treason against the King committed, his lands, livings, and offices were
given of the King's liberality to Macbeth [I.iii.105—11].

"The same night after, at supper, Banquo jested with him and said,
'Now, Macbeth, thou hast obtained those things which the two former
sisters prophesied; there remaineth only for thee to purchase that

which the third said should come to pass' [II.i.21]. Whereupon Macbeth, revolving the thing in his mind, began even then to devise how he might attain to the kingdom; but yet he thought with himself that he must tarry a time, which should advance him thereto (by the Divine Providence) as it had come to pass in his former preferment. But shortly after, it chanced that King Duncan, having two sons by his wife, which was the daughter of Siward, Earl of Northumberland [V.ii.2], he made the elder of them, called Malcolm, Prince of Cumberland, as it were thereby to appoint him his successor in the kingdom immediately after his decease [I.iv.37—9]. Macbeth, sore troubled herewith, for that he saw by this his hope sore hindered [I.iv.48—50] (where, by the old laws of the realm, the ordinance was that if he that should succeed were not of able age to take the charge upon himself, he that was next of blood unto him should be admitted) he began to take counsel how he might usurp the kingdom by force, having a just quarrel so to do (as he took the matter) for that Duncan did what in him lay to defraud him of all manner of title and claim, which he might in time to come pretend [i.e., claim for the crown].

"The words of the three sisters also (of whom before ye have heard) greatly encouraged him hereunto, but specially his wife lay sore upon him to attempt the thing, as she that was very ambitious, burning in unquenchable desire to bear the name of a queen [I.v]. At length, therefore, communicating his purposed intent with his trusty friends, amongst whom Banquo was the chiefest, upon confidence of their promised aid [II.i.25], he slew the King at Inverness, or (as some say) at Botgosuane, in the sixth year of his reign. Then, having a company about him of such as he had made privy to his enterprise, he caused himself to be proclaimed King, and forthwith went unto Scone, where (by common consent) he received the investiture of the kingdom according to the accustomed manner [II.iv.31—2]. The body of Duncan was first conveyed unto Elgin, and there buried in kingly wise; but afterwards it was removed and conveyed unto Colmekill, and there laid in a sepulture amongst his predecessors [II.iv.33—4], in the year after the birth of Our Saviour 1046.

"Malcolm Canmore and Donald Bain, the sons of King Duncan, for fear of their lives (which they might well know that Macbeth would seek to bring to end for his more sure confirmation in the estate) fled into Cumberland [II.iv.25—6], where Malcolm remained till time that Saint Edward, the son of Etheldred, recovered the dominion of England from the Danish power, the which Edward received Malcolm by way of most friendly entertainment [III.vi.26—7], but Donald passed over into Ireland."

Thereafter, says Holinshed, Macbeth maintained justice, punished abuses due to the feeble administration of Duncan, introduced reforms, and reigned well for ten years. Among the thanes punished by death in this period were Ross and Caithness. Holinshed then relates the death of Banquo; see Act III, scene i, and Act III, scene iii.

"Shortly after, he began to show what he was; instead of equity practicing cruelty. For the prick of conscience (as it chanceth ever in tyrants . . .) caused him ever to fear, lest he should be served of the same cup as he had ministered to his predecessor. The words also of the three Weird Sisters would not out of his mind, which, as they promised him the kingdom, so likewise did they promise it at the same time unto the posterity of Banquo [III.i.3—6, 58—59]. He willed therefore the same Banquo, with his son named Fleance, to come to supper that he had prepared for them [III.i.11—15], which was indeed, as he had devised, present death at the hands of certain murderers, whom he had hired to execute that deed, appointing them to meet with the same Banquo and his son without the palace, as they returned to their lodgings, and there to slay them, so that he would not have his house slandered, but that, in time to come, he might clear himself if anything were laid to his charge upon any suspicion that might arise. It chanced yet by the benefit of the dark night, that though the father were slain, the son yet by the help of Almighty God reserving him to better fortune, escaped that danger . . . whereupon to avoid further peril he fled into Wales."

Holinshed goes on to trace the descent of the Stuart dynasty of Scotland from Fleance, through his descendant Walter Steward, who married a daughter of Robert the Bruce, to the sequence of kings named James. Then he takes up the story of Macbeth again; this next passage relates chiefly to Act III, scene iv, Act IV, scene i, and Act IV, scene ii.

"After the contrived slaughter of Banquo, nothing prospered with the foresaid Macbeth: for in manner every man began to doubt [i.e., fear for] his own life and durst unneth [i.e., scarcely] appear in the King's presence; and even as there were many that stood in fear of him, so likewise stood he in fear of many, in such sort that he began to make those away, by one surmised cavillation or other, whom he thought most able to work him any displeasure.

"At length, he found such sweetness by putting his nobles thus to death, that his earnest thirst after blood in this behalf might in no wise be satisfied [III.iv.135—7]. . . . Further, to the end he might the more cruelly oppress his subjects with all tyrantlike wrongs, he built a strong castle on top of a high hill called Dunsinane, situate in Gowrie [V.ii.12], ten miles from Perth. . . . Macbeth, being once determined to have the work go forward, caused the thanes of each shire within the realm to come and help towards that building, each man his course about.

"At the last, when the turn fell unto Macduff, Thane of Fife, to build his part, he sent workmen with all needful provision, and . . . came not himself as others had done, which he refused to do [III.vi.39–43], for doubt lest the King, bearing him (as he partly understood) no great good will, would lay violent hands upon him as he had done upon divers others. . . . Macbeth . . . was sore offended and said, 'I perceive this man will never obey my commandments till he be ridden with a snaffle: but I shall provide well enough for him.' Neither could he afterwards abide to look upon the said Macduff . . . for that he had learned of certain wizards, in whose words he put great confidence (for that the prophecy had happened so right, which the three fairies, or Weird Sisters, had declared unto him) that he ought to take heed of Macduff [IV.i.70–71], who in time to come should seek to destroy him.

"And surely hereupon had he put Macduff to death but that a certain witch, whom he had in great trust, had told that he should never be slain with man born of any woman [IV.i.79–80], nor vanquished till the Wood of Birnam came to the castle of Dunsinane [IV.i.91–3]. By this prophecy Macbeth put all fear out of his heart, supposing he might do what he would. . . . At length Macduff, to avoid peril of life, purposed with himself to pass into England, to procure Malcolm Canmore to claim the crown of Scotland. But this was not so secretly devised by Macduff, but that Macbeth had knowledge given him thereof. . . . For Macbeth had in every nobleman's house one sly fellow or other in fee with him [III.iv.130–1] to reveal all that was said or done within the same, by which sleight he oppressed the most part of the nobles of his realm.

"Immediately then, being advertised whereabout Macduff went, he came hastily with a great power into Fife, and forthwith besieged the castle where Macduff dwelt, trusting to have found him therein. They that kept the house, without any resistance opened the gates and suffered him to enter, mistrusting none evil. But nevertheless Macbeth most cruelly caused the wife and children of Macduff, with all others whom he found in that castle, to be slain. Also he confiscated the goods of Macduff, proclaimed him traitor, and confined him out of all parts of his realm."

Macduff goes to England, where he speaks to Malcolm; their conversation in Act IV, scene iii of the play is based on the speeches Holinshed attributes to them:

"He declared into what great misery the estate of Scotland was brought by the detestable cruelties exercised by the tyrant Macbeth, having committed many horrible slaughters and murders, both as well of the nobles as commons, for the which he was hated right mortally of his liege people, desiring nothing more than to be delivered of that intolerable and most heavy yoke of thraldom. . . .

"Malcolm, hearing Macduff's words . . . fetched a deep sigh, which Macduff perceiving began to fall most earnestly in hand with him to enterprise the delivering of the Scottish people out of the hands of so cruel and bloody a tyrant . . . which was an easy matter for him to bring to pass, considering not only the good title he had, but also the earnest desire of the people to have some occasion ministered whereby they might be revenged of those notable injuries which they daily sustained. . . . Though Malcolm was very sorrowful for the oppression of his countrymen the Scots, in manner as Macduff had declared, yet doubting whether he were come as one that meant unfeignedly as he spake, or else sent from Macbeth to betray him, he thought to have some further trial, and thereupon dissembling his mind at the first, he answered as followeth:

" 'I am truly very sorry for the misery chanced to my country of Scotland, but though I have never so great affection to relieve the same, yet by reason of certain incurable vices which reign in me [IV.iii.50—51], I am nothing meet thereto. First, such immoderate lust and voluptuous sensuality (the abominable fountain of all vices) followeth me, that if I were made King of Scots, I should seek to deflower your maids and matrons, in such wise that mine intemperancy should be more importable [i.e., unbearable] unto you than the bloody tyranny of Macbeth now is' [IV.iii.57—66]. Hereunto Macduff answered, 'This surely is a very evil fault, for many noble princes and kings have lost both lives and kingdoms for the same; nevertheless there are women enough in Scotland, and therefore follow my counsel. Make thyself King, and I shall convey the matter so wisely, that thou shalt be so satisfied at thy pleasure in such secret wise, that no man shall be aware thereof' [IV.iii.66—76].

"Then said Malcolm, 'I am also the most avaricious creature on the earth, so that if I were King, I should seek so many ways to get lands and goods that I would slay the most part of all the nobles of Scotland by surmised accusations, to the end I might enjoy their lands, goods and possessions' [IV.iii.76—84]. . . . 'Therefore,' saith Malcolm, 'suffer me to remain where I am, lest if I attain to the regiment of your realm, mine inquenchable avarice [IV.iii.78] may prove such that ye would think the displeasures which now grieve you should seem easy in respect of the unmeasurable outrage which might ensue through my coming amongst you.'

"Macduff to this made answer, how it was a far worse fault than the other: for avarice is the root of all mischief, and for that crime the most part of our kings have been slain and brought to their final end. 'Yet, notwithstanding, follow my counsel, and take upon thee the crown. There is gold and riches enough in Scotland to satisfy thy greedy desire' [IV.iii.84—90]. Then said Malcolm again, 'I am furthermore inclined to dissimulation, telling of leasings [i.e., falsehoods], and all other kinds of deceit, so that I naturally rejoice in nothing so much as to betray and deceive such as put any trust or confidence in my words. Then sith there is nothing that more becometh a prince than constancy, verity, truth and justice, with all other laudable fellowship of those fair and noble virtues which are comprehended in soothfastness [i.e., truthfulness], and that lying utterly overthroweth the same, you see how unable I am to govern any province or region . . .' [IV.iii.91—100].

"Then said Macduff, 'This yet is the worst of all, and there I leave thee, and therefore say, O ye unhappy and miserable Scottishmen, which are thus scourged with so many and sundry calamities, each one above another: ye have one cursed and wicked tyrant that now reigneth over you, without any right or title, oppressing you with his most bloody cruelty. The other, that hath the right to the crown, is so replete with the inconstant behaviour and manifest vices of Englishmen, that he is nothing worthy to enjoy it: for by his own confession he is not only avaricious, and given to unsatiable lust, but so false a traitor withal that no trust is to be had unto any word he speaketh. Adieu, Scotland, for now I account myself a banished man forever, without comfort or consolation.' And with those words the brackish tears trickled down his cheeks very abundantly [IV.iii.100—14].

"At the last, when he was ready to depart, Malcolm took him by the sleeve, and said, 'Be of good comfort, Macduff, for I have none of these vices before remembered, but have jested with thee in this manner only to prove thy mind: for divers times heretofore hath Macbeth sought by this manner of means to bring me into his hands. . . .' Incontinently hereupon they embraced each other, and promising to be faithful the one to the other, they fell in consultation how they might best provide for all their business, to bring the same to good effect."

Holinshed says that Macduff went to the borders of Scotland and wrote letters to Scottish nobles urging them to take sides with Malcolm and himself:

"In the meantime, Malcolm purchased such favour at King Edward's hands, that old Siward, Earl of Northumberland was appointed with ten thousand men to go with him into Scotland to support him in this enterprise for recovery of his right [IV.iii.134]."

The nobles of Scotland, says Holinshed, now divided into two factions, one supporting Malcolm, one Macbeth; but as Malcolm's power increased, Macbeth withdrew to Dunsinane, intending there "to fight with his enemies, if they meant to pursue him." The battle scenes of Act V are developed from the following passages in Holinshed:

"Malcolm following hastily after Macbeth, came the night before the battle unto Birnam Wood, and when his army had rested a while there to refresh them, he commanded every man to get a bough of some tree or other of that wood in his hand, as big as he might bear, and to march forth therewith in such wise, that on the next morrow they might come closely and without sight in this manner within view of his enemies [V.iv.4—7]. On the morrow, when Macbeth beheld them coming in this sort, he first marvelled what the matter meant, but in the end remembered himself that the prophecy which he had heard long before that time, of the coming of Birnam Wood to Dunsinane Castle, was likely to be now fulfilled [V.v.33—46]. Nevertheless, he brought his men in order of battle and exhorted them to do valiantly; howbeit his enemies had scarcely cast from them their boughs, when Macbeth, perceiving their numbers, betook him straight to flight, whom Macduff pursued with great hatred even till he came unto Lumphinnans, where Macbeth, perceiving that Macduff was hard at his back, leapt beside his horse, saying, 'Thou traitor, what meaneth it that thou shouldest thus in vain follow me, that am not appointed to be slain by any creature that is born of a woman? Come on, therefore, and receive thy reward which thou hast deserved for thy pains' [V.vii.37—42]. And therewithal, he lifted up his sword, thinking to have slain him.

"But Macduff, quickly avoiding from his horse, yet he came at him, answered (with his naked sword in his hand) saying, 'It is true, Macbeth, and now shall thine insatiable cruelty have an end, for I am even he that thy wizards have told thee of, who was never born of my mother, but ripped out of her womb' [V.vii.42—5]. Therewithal he stept unto him and slew him in that place. Then, cutting his head from his shoulders, he set it upon a pole and brought it unto Malcolm [V.viii.20—21]."

This was the end of Macbeth, says Holinshed, after a reign of seventeen years, which began well but degenerated when Macbeth succumbed to "illusion of the Devil." Malcolm was crowned, called a parliament, and rewarded his followers:

"He created many earls, lords, barons, and knights. Many of them that before were thanes were at this time made earls, as Fife, Menteith, Atholl, Lennox, Murray, Caithness, Ross and Angus. These were the first earls that have been heard of amongst the Scottishmen [V.viii.-28—30]. . . . Many new surnames were taken up at this time amongst them, as . . . Seiton . . . with many other that had possessions given them, which gave names to the owners for the time [V.iii.19].

Elsewhere, in his history of England, Holinshed describes the death of Siward's son, reported in *Macbeth* in Act V, scene viii:

"It is recorded also that in the foresaid battle, in which Earl Siward vanquished the Scots, one of Siward's sons chanced to be slain, whereof, although the father had good cause to be sorrowful, yet when he heard that he died of a wound which he had received in fighting stoutly in the forepart of his body and that with his face towards the enemy, he greatly rejoiced thereat to hear that he died so manfully. . . . 'I rejoice,' saith he, 'even with all my heart, for I would not wish either to my son nor to myself any other kind of death.' "

Holinshed also describes King Edward the Confessor in terms echoed in the play, IV.iii.146—59:

"As hath been thought, he was inspired with the gift of prophecy, and also to have had the gift of healing infirmities and diseases. He used to help those that were vexed with the disease commonly called the King's Evil, and left that virtue, as it were a portion of inheritance, unto his successors, the kings of this realm."

Shakespeare's version of the murder of Duncan is based on Holinshed's account of the murder of King Duff by Donwald. This followed on Duff's punishing of noblemen, including kinsmen of Donwald, for conspiring with witches against him. Donwald was urged by his wife to seek revenge, and the following passage suggested to Shakespeare much of the action from Act I, scene v to Act II, scene iv:

"Through the setting-on of his wife, and in revenge of such un-
thankfulness, he found means to murder the King within the foresaid
castle of Forres, where he used to sojourn. For the King, being in that
country, was accustomed to lie most commonly within the same castle,
having a special trust in Donwald, as a man whom he never suspected
[I.iv.11—14].

"But Donwald . . . could not but show manifest tokens of great
grief at home amongst his family, which his wife perceiving ceased
not to travail with him till she understood what was the cause of his
displeasure. Which at length, when she had learned by his own relation, she . . . counselled him (sith the King oftentimes used to lodge in
his house without any guard about him other than the garrison of the
castle, which was wholly at his commandment) to make him away and
showed him the means whereby he might soonest accomplish it.

"Donwald, thus being the more kindled in wrath by the words of
his wife, determined to follow her advice in the execution of so heinous
an act. . . . It chanced that the King upon the day before he purposed to
depart forth of the castle was long in his oratory at his prayers, and
there continued till it was late in the night. At the last, coming forth,
he called such afore him as had faithfully served him . . . and, giving
them hearty thanks, he bestowed sundry honourable gifts amongst
them, of the which number Donwald was one . . . [II.i.13—15].

"At length . . . he got him into his privy chamber, only with two of
his chamberlains, who, having brought him to bed, came forth again
and then fell to banqueting with Donwald and his wife, who had prepared divers delicate dishes and sundry sorts of drinks for their rear-
supper or collation, whereat they sat up so long till they had charged
their stomachs with such full gorges that their heads were no sooner
got to the pillow but asleep they were so fast that a man might have
removed the chamber over them sooner than to have awaked them out
of their drunken sleep [II.ii.5—8].

"Then Donwald, though he abhorred the act greatly in his heart,
yet, through instigation of his wife, he called four of his servants unto
him . . . and speedily going about the murder, they entered the chamber
in which the King lay a little before cock's crow, where they secretly
cut his throat as he lay sleeping, without any busking [i.e., prepara-
tion] at all; and immediately, by a postern gate, they carried forth the
dead body into the fields. . . . In the morning, when the noise was
raised in the King's chamber how the King was slain, his body conveyed away, and the bed all berayed [i.e., stained] with blood, he,
Donwald, with the watch ran thither as though he had known nothing

of the matter, and breaking into the chamber and finding cakes of blood in the bed and on the floor about the sides of it, he forthwith slew the chamberlain, as guilty of that heinous murder . . . [II.iii. 92—101].

"Finally, such was his overearnest diligence in the severe inquisition and trial of the offenders herein that some of the lords began to mislike the matter and to smell forth shrewd tokens that he should not be altogether clear himself [III.i.2—3; III.vi.1—16]. But for so much as they were in that country where he had the whole rule, what by reason of his friends and authority together, they doubted to utter what they thought till time and place should serve thereunto, and hereupon got them away, every man to his home. For the space of six months together after this heinous murder thus committed, there appeared no sun by day, nor moon by night, in any part of the realm, but still was the sky covered with continual clouds, and sometimes such outrageous winds arose, with lightnings and tempests, that the people were in great fear of present destruction . . . [II.iii.47—54].

"Monstrous sights also that were seen within the Scottish kingdom that year were there: horses in Lothian, being of singular beauty and swiftness, did eat their own flesh and would in no wise taste any other meat. . . . There was a sparrowhawk also strangled by an owl . . . all men understood that the abominable murder of King Duff was the cause hereof [II.iv.1—20]."

APPENDIX C

A Note on Shakespeare's English

Elizabethan English is sufficiently like that of the present day to appear at first sight modern except in a few eccentricities of usage and spelling, and this is a major reason why Shakespeare's plays have remained so readily accessible to later ages. However, the development of modern standard English came about gradually as a process not completed before the eighteenth century. In Shakespeare's time the language was more fluid, more experimental, than it is now. The process of standardizing had begun to gather momentum under the influence of the printed books that circulated in steadily increasing numbers after William Caxton brought printing to England about 1474.

Books bred literacy, but although by 1600 perhaps half the population may have been able to read, there were no newspapers or other modern means of spreading information, and Shakespeare wrote for an audience that obtained its news, its entertainment, and its instruction (in sermons, for instance) largely through the ear.

Many literate Englishmen debated in the sixteenth century whether their language was rich or "copious" enough to serve literature at a time when Latin was still a common language of European culture. The debate was effectively settled by the flowering of the English drama between 1580 and 1620, a period roughly coinciding with Shakespeare's productive life. The dramatists, Shakespeare above all, imported or invented words, ranged freely in metaphor, and bent grammar to their service. They were using a language that as yet lacked formulated rules, and were accustomed to freedoms no longer permissible, as, for example, the very common false concord, where subject and verb do not agree ("Time and the hour runs through the roughest day," I.iii.148), or the use of the nominative case for the objective ("the dead man's knell / Is there scarce asked for who," IV.iii.-170–1). They were also writing for an audience used to listening and ready to seize on nuances of meaning such as the quibble on "cast" meaning both "wrestle" and "vomit" (II.iii.34). Modern readers are not usually on the look-out for open puns, and regard them as a rather dubious form of humor, but the Elizabethan audience would probably have taken a grim pleasure in such a play on words as Lady Macbeth's

> I'll gild the faces of the grooms withal,
> For it must seem their guilt.
>
> II.ii.56—7

In their speech Shakespeare's characters depart from "correct" modern usage in many small ways. It is not merely that certain forms now archaic were still common, like the use of the second person pronoun, "thou," in familiar relationships, but also that the Elizabethans had little regard for consistency or regularity, and would use, for example, "which" for "who" (III.i.76), the present tense for the past ("Fleance is 'scaped," III.iv.19), and the plural for the singular ("there arc a crew," IV.iii.141). They were free with negatives, often using "nor," for instance, where we would use "and," as in this passage:

> That hast no less deserved, nor must be known
> No less to have done so . . .
>
> I.iv.30—1

They used prepositions with a colloquial freedom now relegated to vulgar speech, especially the common "on" for "of" (as at I.iii.84 "eaten on the insane root," and V.i.51), and made them serve in constructions no longer familiar, like "blame / His pestered senses to recoil and start" (V.ii.22–3), where we would say "for recoiling and starting."

Perhaps most of these differences cause little trouble to the modern reader or audience, since in many cases the meaning is clear enough, and some Elizabethan usages remain alive in modern colloquial English. Many of the words invented or first recorded by Shakespeare and other writers of his age have passed into common currency, but some of their coinages failed to survive, like *compunctious* (I.v.43), meaning "remorseful," and *intrenchant* (V.vii.38), meaning "incapable of being cut." Others, like *disseat* (V.iii.21) or the compound words *rump-fed* (I.iii.6) and *lily-livered* (V.iii.15), are very effective as images in the context for which they were invented, but have not achieved an independent life. Less obvious and perhaps more difficult to cope with are the many words whose meanings have changed over the centuries, or whose original meaning has dwindled into a secondary sense, as *division* (IV.iii.96) meaning "variation" as in music, *modern* (IV.iii.170) meaning "commonplace," or *luxurious* (IV.iii.58) meaning "lecherous." Some words have fallen out of use: for example, *mated* (V.i.66), meaning "baffled" (this survives as a technical term in the game of chess); *trains* (IV.iii.118), meaning "snares"; and *unrough* (V.ii.10), meaning "beardless." Other words in use in Shakespeare's age show their character as borrowed terms, sometimes of French origin, like *compt* (I.vi.26), *Hautboys* (I.vii, stage direction; changed to the modern *Oboes* in this edition), *gouts* (II.i.46; French *gouttes*), *convince* (I.vii.65; Latin *convincere*). Often words that are familiar now in everyday usage possess quite a different sense in *Macbeth*; examples are *dismal* (III.v.21), meaning "calamitous," from the Latin *dies mali* (evil days); *fact* (III.vi.10), meaning "evil deed," from the Latin *facere* (to make or do); and *still* (V.vii.43), meaning "always."

Shakespeare's vocabulary was, in any case, an unusually rich one, both because of his inventiveness with compounds, prefixes (*dis-seat*), and suffixes (*confine-less*, IV.iii.55), and because of his ready familiarity with areas of experience that remain obscure to most people today (note, for instance, his use of legal terms like *affeered* [IV.iii.34] or *fee-grief* [IV.iii.196]).

Possibly the least obvious difference between Shakespeare's English and modern English lies in its pronunciation. Sometimes in the orig-

inal text, spellings that had not yet reached a fixed and final form indicated a pronunciation, like *murthered* for *murdered* (III.i.65), or
diminitive for *diminutive* (IV.ii.10)—both modernized in this edition
—and sometimes a rhyme or a pun is revealing. Many Elizabethan
words are accented on different syllables than would be normal in
modern speech; actors sometimes miss the correct accent in performance, but the meter usually makes it clear, as in *pur'vey·or* (I.vi.22),
ba'boon's (IV.i.37), and *per·se've·rance* (IV.iii.93). Meter may also
indicate where words are lengthened in pronunciation, like *preparation* (I.v.31; five syllables), *monst(e)rous* (III.vi.8), *rememb(e)rance*
(III.ii.30), in which the *e* that originally preceded the final syllable is
sounded. Words that are contracted, like *devil* (IV.iii.56), pronounced
"de'il," can also often be discovered from the meter. In general con-
sonants were pronounced as they are now, except that some which are
now silent were still sounded, like the *k* in *knight*, and the *g* in *gnaw*.
Some vowel sounds were different, and in diphthongs like *ea* as in
treat or *dear*, both vowels were heard—as they still are in the regional
speech of northeast England. An approximate idea of the sound of
Shakespeare's English can be gained by listening to such a marked
British regional accent. The record *Beowulf, Chaucer, Shakespeare
and the Gettysburg Address* (National Council of Teachers of English,
RL 20—7) contains speeches from *Hamlet* and *The Merchant of Venice*
read in an Elizabethan accent.

APPENDIX D

MACBETH *at the Globe in 1611*

In the spring of 1611, Simon Forman, an astrologer, saw a performance
of *Macbeth* at the Globe Theatre and afterward wrote a description of
it. His memory of what he saw seems to have been affected by memories of what he had read in Holinshed, for he describes the Witches
in Holinshed's language as "women fairies or nymphs." He also confused events in his mind, for he wrote that Macbeth went to Inverness
at Duncan's bidding, with "the Prince of Northumberland." However,
it is interesting to note what did impress Forman, namely the Witches
and their prophecies, the guilty conscience of Macbeth after the murder
of Duncan, the banquet and sleepwalking scenes. He does not men-

tion the apparitions of Act IV, scene i, and dismisses the end of the play in a sentence. In other words, he seems to have been more affected by the play's inner action than by its melodramatic events, and this may be a pointer to a simplicity in the staging of the play at the Globe. Only once does Forman describe a piece of stage business, and it is in connection with the Ghost of Banquo:

The next night, being at supper with his noblemen whom he had bid to a feast to the which also Banquo should have come, he began to speak of noble Banquo, and to wish that he were there. And as he thus did, standing up to drink a carouse to him, the ghost of Banquo came and sat down in his chair behind him. And he, turning about to sit down again, saw the ghost of Banquo, which fronted him so that he fell into a great passion of fear and fury, uttering many words about his murder, by which, when they heard that Banquo was murdered, they suspected Macbeth.

This passage also makes clear that at the Globe the Ghost of Banquo was represented by an actor, not left to the audience's imagination as has been done in some modern productions.

The manuscript of Simon Forman's notes is preserved in the Bodleian Library, Oxford, and reprinted, with Forman's very individual spelling, by E. K. Chambers in *William Shakespeare* (1930), II, 337—8.

APPENDIX E

Textual Problems and the Witches' Songs

Two features of the Folio text of *Macbeth* have puzzled scholars. One is the interpolation in Act III, scene v and Act IV, scene i of the first lines of two songs from *The Witch*, a play by Thomas Middleton of uncertain date, but probably written between 1609 and 1615; indeed, many scholars think that the whole of Act III, scene v and parts of Act IV, scene i were inserted into the play to soften and make more diverting the Witch scenes, and they argue that Middleton wrote these passages. It should be noted that Shakespeare's Hecate, a goddess in *Macbeth*, is very different from Hecate in *The Witch*, where she is merely chief witch; that there is no resemblance to *The Witch*, or to

Middleton's style of writing, in the passages regarded as interpolations; and that the songs in *The Witch* are irrelevant not only to *Macbeth* as a whole, but also to Act III, scene v and the passages thought to be added in Act IV, scene i. (On this matter, see W. W. Greg, *The Shakespeare First Folio* [Oxford, 1955], pp. 390–2 and p. 397.) The length of the disputed passages is about 50 lines (III.v; IV.i.39–43 and 124–31); the verse in them tends to be iambic rather than trochaic as in the main dialogue of the Witches, and Hecate appears only in these lines. However, Act III, scene v serves the purpose of contrasting Macbeth's belief that he commands the Witches (III.iv.-131–4) with their certainty that they control him (III.v.26–31), and can be defended as functional in providing a preparation for Act IV, scene i. The argument is not yet finally settled.

The first song refers by name to witches (Stadlin and Hoppo) who are characters in the scene (III.iii) of *The Witch*, and requires a "spirit like a cat" to appear. The second song is sung by Hecate, several witches, and her son Firestone. It is difficult to see how these could ever have been incorporated into *Macbeth* without considerable alteration. To show its remoteness from Shakespeare's play, the text of one song is reprinted below. The text of the songs was first printed in a quarto of *Macbeth* published in 1673, and in a much altered version of *Macbeth* by Sir William D'Avenant that appeared in 1674. Middleton's play remained in manuscript until the late eighteenth century, and has been most recently edited by W. W. Greg and F. P. Wilson for Malone Society Reprints, 1948 (1950). D'Avenant's version of *Macbeth* has recently been edited, from a manuscript in Yale University Library, by Christopher Spencer (New Haven, 1961). The following song seems to be that called for in *Macbeth* (IV.i.43) under the heading "Black spirits":

Hecate:	Black spirits and white, red spirits and grey,
	Mingle, mingle, mingle, you that mingle may!
	Titty, Tiffin,
	Keep it stiff in;
	Firedrake, Puckey,
	Make it lucky;
	Liard, Robin,
	You must bob in.
	Round, around, around, about, about!
	All ill come running in, all good keep out!
First Witch:	Here's the blood of a bat.
Hecate:	Put in that, O put in that!

Second Witch:	Here's libbard's-bane.
Hecate:	Put in again.
First Witch:	The juice of toad, the oil of adder.
Second Witch:	Those will make the younker sadder.
Hecate:	Put in—there's all—and rid the stench.
Firestone:	Nay, here's three ounces of the red-haired wench.
All the Witches:	Round, around, around, etc.

For the song "Come away," a musical setting (probably by Shakespeare's contemporary Robert Johnson) survives. Some of the music for D'Avenant's version of *Macbeth* was written by the late-seventeenth-century composer Matthew Locke. Well-known modern composers who have written incidental music for the play include Khatchaturian, Darius Milhaud, and William Walton. Many other composers have written music on the theme of the play, among them Smetana, Richard Strauss, and Michael Tippett. Several attempts have been made to make an opera out of the action, and two distinguished works have resulted, Verdi's *Macbeth* (1847; revised 1865), and Ernest Bloch's *Macbeth* (1910). For further comment on music in *Macbeth*, see *Shakespeare in Music*, edited by Phyllis Hartnoll (London, 1964), and F. W. Sternfeld, *Music in Shakespearean Tragedy* (London, 1963).

The other feature of *Macbeth* which has given rise to much speculation is its brevity, for it is, with the exception of *The Comedy of Errors*, the shortest of Shakespeare's plays. The presence of what seem to be additions in the text has encouraged critics to look also for cuts. The irregularity of the verse in scenes like I.ii, and sudden changes of direction or pace (see, for example, I.ii.38–42) have been seen as evidence of abridgment, but can be defended as appropriate to the action—in this case the hasty and disjointed message of the bleeding Captain. Again, at I.vii.47, Lady Macbeth's words

> What beast was't then
> That made you break this enterprise to me?

have led some editors to argue that Macbeth must have discussed with his wife the murder of Duncan in a scene later cut and now lost. However, the action is perfectly coherent without any such scene, and, indeed, there is no need to assume cutting as an explanation for textual difficulties.

It is generally agreed that *Macbeth* was printed from a manuscript that had been used in the theater, or from a transcript of such a manuscript. There are not many direct indications of derivation from a playing script, but perhaps the strongest is at II.iii.80, where a stage direction, "Ring the bell," appears to have been incorporated into a line of verse by the printer (see the note to this passage). As a whole the text seems fairly free from corruption, and one scholar (Richard Flatter, *Shakespeare's Producing Hand*, 1948) has even claimed that it shows Shakespeare's own arrangement. No one else accepts this view, for it conflicts with all that is known of the play's textual history, and with the normal practice in the Elizabethan theater and printing house, but at least his theory underlines the coherence of this particular text.

APPENDIX F

Bibliography

Some idea of the vast array of writings about Shakespeare may be gained by glancing through the relevant sections in *The Cambridge Bibliography of English Literature*, ed. F. W. Bateson (4 vols., Cambridge, England, 1941), which has a *Supplement*, ed. G. W. Watson (1957). More recent work is listed in the Annual Bibliographies of *Shakespeare Quarterly* and *PMLA.* The New Variorum edition of *Macbeth* was first published in 1873, and the revised edition of 1903, ed. H. H. Furness Jr., is now available in paperback (New York: Dover, 1963). This has a bibliography relating specifically to the play, and later studies of *Macbeth* can be traced by consulting *A Shakespeare Bibliography*, by W. Ebisch and L. L. Schücking (2 vols., Oxford, 1930, 1936), or scholarly editions such as the new Arden, ed. Kenneth Muir (London, 1951), or the New Cambridge, ed. J. Dover Wilson (Cambridge, England, 1949). An excellent critical survey of "The Year's Contributions to Shakespearian Study" has appeared annually since 1948 in *Shakespeare Survey*, ed. Allardyce Nicoll (Cambridge, England).

There is much useful and attractively presented material on the general background of Shakespeare's age in the well-illustrated *Shakespeare's England*, ed. Sir Sidney Lee and C. T. Onions (2 vols., Oxford, 1916), and in *Shakespeare in his Own Age* (*Shakespeare Survey*, 17, ed. Allardyce Nicoll, Cambridge, England, 1964). J. Dover Wilson's more compact collection of extracts from writings of Shakespeare's age, *Life in Shakespeare's England* (London: Pelican, 1944), provides a ready insight into the period. The political history of the age is dealt with concisely in the relevant volumes in the Pelican History of England, *England under the Tudors*, by S. T. Bindoff (London: Penguin, 1950), and in *England in the Seventeenth Century*, by Maurice Ashley (London: Penguin, 3rd edn., 1961).

The standard reference work on the history of the theater is E. K. Chambers, *The Elizabethan Stage* (4 vols., Oxford, 1923). Briefer and more readable general works are G. B. Harrison's *Elizabethan Plays and Players* (Ann Arbor, 1956) and A. Harbage's *Shakespeare's Audience* (New York, 1941). *Shakespeare's Stage*, by A. Nagler (New Haven, 1958) is an excellent short handbook. The evidence relating to acting, staging, and dramatic practice in general at the Globe Theatre is well presented by Bernard Beckerman in *Shakespeare at the Globe, 1599-1609* (New York, 1962).

The authoritative life of Shakespeare is that by E. K. Chambers: *William Shakespeare. A Study of Facts and Problems* (2 vols., Oxford, 1930). A shorter and more up-to-date study is G. E. Bentley's *William Shakespeare, A Biographical Handbook* (New Haven, 1961). A good general account of Shakespeare's work is given in *An Approach to Shakespeare*, by D. A. Traversi (1938; New York: Anchor, 1956).

Of the many books on Shakespeare's tragedies, a few stand out as especially representative of one line of thought. Still the most incisive analysis of the characters in action is A. C. Bradley's *Shakespearean Tragedy* (London, 1904), but the critique of Bradley in J. I. M. Stewart's *Character and Motive in Shakespeare* (London, 1949) is worth study. A seminal account of the plays in terms of themes and imagery was G. Wilson Knight's *The Wheel of Fire* (London, 1930; revised edition 1949; see also his *The Imperial Theme*, 1931—reissued London, 1963 —on "life themes" in *Macbeth*), but a less heady study is available in L. C. Knights' *Some Shakespearean Themes* (London, 1959). G. B. Harrison's account of *Macbeth* in *Shakespeare's Tragedies* (London, 1951) as the weakest of Shakespeare's tragedies serves as a corrective to extravagant praise. More recently, John Holloway has written a contentious but stimulating attack on reading the tragedies for "themes" or morals in his *The Story of the Night* (London, 1961).

The framework of conventions within which Shakespeare wrote his tragedies is examined in E. E. Stoll's *Art and Artifice in Shakespeare* (Cambridge, England, reprinted 1938) and Muriel Bradbrook's *Themes and Conventions of Elizabethan Tragedy* (Cambridge, England, 1935). Another important study of the ideas of tragedy inherited by Shakespeare's age is Willard Farnham's *The Medieval Heritage of Elizabethan Tragedy* (1936; reprinted Oxford, 1956). An excellent brief essay on the character of Shakespeare's later plays is Maynard Mack's "The Jacobean Shakespeare" in *Jacobean Theatre*, ed. J. R. Brown and B. Harris (London, 1960).

Some interesting early essays on *Macbeth* are readily available: Thomas Whately's comparison of Richard III and Macbeth, and Thomas De Quincey's essay "On the Knocking at the Gate in *Macbeth*" are both reprinted in *Shakespeare Criticism*, ed. D. Nichol Smith (Oxford, 1916). Other early comments on the play, including the actress Mrs. Sarah Siddons' account of her interpretation of Lady Macbeth, are reprinted in the New Variorum edition. There are numerous modern studies of the play. Some have a special interest, as treating particularly well or exhaustively a certain approach to the problems of *Macbeth*. The demonology and supernatural aspects are best discussed in W. C. Curry's *Shakespeare's Philosophical Patterns* (Baton Rouge, 1937). The circumstances of the play's composition and first production are examined at length in H. N. Paul's *The Royal Play of Macbeth* (New York, 1950), an interesting book although the author tends to too much speculation on slender evidence. The imagery of the play has been much examined, and two full-length examinations of it scene by scene, both by commentators with a strong Christian leaning, discuss the poetry in some detail; the first of these, *The Time is Free*, by Roy Walker (London, 1949), is very much better than the second, G. R. Elliott's *Dramatic Providence in Macbeth* (Princeton, 1958).

However, the language of the play and its poetic texture have perhaps been most incisively discussed in shorter essays; among the best are those by L. C. Knights, "How Many Children Had Lady Macbeth?" (1933; reprinted in *Explorations*, London, 1946) a title ironically alluding to the kind of question Bradley raised; by Cleanth Brooks, "The Naked Babe and the Cloak of Manliness," in *The Well Wrought Urn* (New York, 1947); and by M. M. Mahood in *Shakespeare's Wordplay* (London, 1957). A seminal study of poetic imagery was Caroline Spurgeon's essay in her *Shakespeare's Imagery* (Cambridge, England, 1935); the image clusters in *Macbeth* are discussed in E. A. Armstrong's *Shakespeare's Imagination* (1946; London, reissued 1963). Macbeth himself is compared with Richard III in E. M. W. Tillyard's treatment of the play as one of *Shakespeare's History Plays* (New York, 1946), and with Brutus in G. Wilson Knight's essay on his character in *The Wheel of Fire*. The relation of Macbeth to the tragedies written after it, *Timon of Athens, Antony and Cleopatra* and *Coriolanus*, is discussed in Willard Farnham's *Shakespeare's Tragic Frontier* (Berkeley, 1950). *Shakespeare Survey*, 19, ed. Kenneth Muir (Cambridge, 1966) takes

Macbeth as its main theme, and contains several essays on the play. Finally, a useful elementary critical introduction is provided by John Russell Brown in Shakespeare: *The Tragedy of Macbeth* (London, 1963).

The sources of the play are discussed in most of the editions available, but two valuable essays on this topic are those by M. C. Bradbrook in *Shakespeare Survey*, 4 (Cambridge, 1951), and by Kenneth Muir in his *Shakespeare's Sources*, Vol. I: "Comedies and Tragedies" (London, 1957). A definitive account of the sources, and a full reprint, will soon be available when Geoffrey Bullough completes his edition of *Narrative and Dramatic Sources of Shakespeare* (London and New York, 1957 onward).

There are various phonograph recordings of *Macbeth*, usually abridged; that of the Marlowe Society (3 records, London 4343; 1316) is complete.

APPENDIX G

Abbreviations, References, and Editions

Abbott	E. A. Abbott, *A Shakespearian Grammar* (1869). References are to sections, not to pages.
All's Well	*All's Well That Ends Well.*
Caesar	*Julius Caesar.*
D'Avenant	*Macbeth,* altered by Sir William D'Avenant (1674), and edited by Christopher Spencer (1961).
Dover Wilson	*Macbeth,* edited by John Dover Wilson (New Cambridge Shakespeare, 1947).
F, F2, F3, F4	The first four collected editions of Shakespeare's plays, published as folios in 1623, 1632, 1664, and 1685.
Hanmer	*Works . . .,* edited by Sir Thomas Hanmer, 6 vols. (1744–46).
Holinshed	Raphael Holinshed, *Chronicles of England, Scotland and Ireland,* 3 vols. (1577; revised 1587).
Johnson	*The Plays of William Shakespeare,* edited by Dr. Samuel Johnson, 8 vols. (1765).

Kittredge	*Macbeth*, edited by G. L. Kittredge (1939).
Lear	*King Lear.*
Merry Wives	*The Merry Wives of Windsor.*
McKerrow	*The Works of Thomas Nashe*, edited by R. B. McKerrow, 5 vols. (1904–10; reissued 1958).
M.N. Dream	*A Midsummer Night's Dream.*
Much Ado	*Much Ado About Nothing.*
Muir	*Macbeth*, edited by Kenneth Muir (new Arden Shakespeare, 1951; revised 1953).
OED	*A New English Dictionary*, edited by J. A. Murray, H. Bradley, W. A. Craigie, and C. T. Onions, 13 vols. (1888–1933).
Onions	C. T. Onions, *A Shakespeare Glossary* (1911; revised edition, 1946).
Pope	*The Works of Shakespeare*, edited by Alexander Pope, 6 vols. (1723–25).
Romeo	*Romeo and Juliet.*
Rowe	*The Works of Mr. William Shakespeare*, edited by Nicholas Rowe, 7 vols. (1709).
S.D.	Stage direction(s).
Steevens	*The Plays of William Shakespeare*, edited by I. Reed (with notes by George Steevens), 15 vols. (1793).
Theobald	*The Works of Shakespeare*, edited by Lewis Theobald, 7 vols. (1733).
Tilley	M. P. Tilley, *A Dictionary of Proverbs in England in the Sixteenth and Seventeenth Centuries* (1950). References are to the initial letter and number by which proverbs are listed, not to pages.
Timon	*Timon of Athens.*
Wright	*Macbeth*, edited by W. A. Wright (Clarendon Shakespeare, 1869).